Workshop on Deep Learning and Formal Languages: Building Bridges

Florence, Italy
2 August 2019

ISBN: 978-1-5108-9118-0

Printed from e-media with permission by:

Curran Associates, Inc.
57 Morehouse Lane
Red Hook, NY 12571

CURRAN ASSOCIATES INC. proceedings.com

Some format issues inherent in the e-media version may also appear in this print version.

Printed by Curran Associates, Inc. (2019)

For permission requests, please contact the Association for Computational Linguistics at the address below.

Association for Computational Linguistics
209 N. Eighth Street
Stroudsburg, Pennsylvania 18360

Phone: 1-570-476-8006
Fax: 1-570-476-0860

acl@aclweb.org

Additional copies of this publication are available from:

Curran Associates, Inc.
57 Morehouse Lane
Red Hook, NY 12571 USA
Phone: 845-758-0400
Fax: 845-758-2633
Email: curran@proceedings.com
Web: www.proceedings.com

ACL 2019

Deep Learning and Formal Languages: Building Bridges

Proceedings of the Workshop

August 2, 2019
Florence, Italy

Introduction

While deep learning and neural networks have revolutionized the field of natural language processing, changed the habits of its practitioners and opened up new research directions, many aspects of the inner workings of deep neural networks remain unknown.

At the same time, we have access to many decades of accumulated knowledge on formal languages, grammar, and transductions, both weighted and unweighted and for strings as well as trees: closure properties, computational complexity of various operations, relationships between various classes of them, and many empirical and theoretical results on their learnability.

The goal of this workshop is to bring researchers together who are interested in how our understanding of formal languages can contribute to the understanding and design of neural network architectures for natural language processing.

All 7 accepted papers and non-archival extended abstracts explore those connections. They do this either by using results from formal languages to improve neural methods or by trying to understand better neural methods through well-studied characteristics from formal languages. Finding such bridges is also the main point of the 6 invited talks.

We would like to thank the authors and specially the programme committee for the timely and insightful reviews. We are looking forward of seeing you in Florence!

The workshop organizers:

Jason Eisner, Matthias Gallé, Jeffrey Heinz, Ariadna Quattoni, Guillaume Rabusseau

Organizers:

Jason Eisner, Johns Hopkins University
Matthias Gallé, Naver Labs Europe
Jeffrey Heinz, Stony Brook University
Ariadna Quattoni, dMetrics
Guillaume Rabusseau, Université de Montréal / Mila

Program Committee:

Raphael Bailly, Université Paris 1
Borja Balle, Amazon
Xavier Carreras, dMetrics
Shay B. Cohen, University of Edinburgh
Alex Clark, University of London
Ewan Dunbar, Université Paris Diderot
Marc Dymetman, Naver Labs Europe
Kyle Gorman, City University of New York
Hadrien Glaude, Amazon
John Hale, University of Georgia
Mans Hulden, University of Colorado
Franco Luque, University of Córdoba
Chihiro Shibata, Tokyo University of Technology
Adina Williams, FAIR

Invited Speaker:

Rémi Eyraud, Aix-Marseilles University
Robert Frank, Yale University
John Kelleher, Technological University Dublin
Kevin Knight, Didi
Ariadna Quattoni, dMetrics
Noah Smith, University of Washington / Allen Institute for Artificial Intelligence

Table of Contents

Sequential Neural Networks as Automata
William Merrill 1

Grammatical Sequence Prediction for Real-Time Neural Semantic Parsing
Chunyang Xiao, Christoph Teichmann and Konstantine Arkoudas 14

Relating RNN Layers with the Spectral WFA Ranks in Sequence Modelling
Farhana Ferdousi Liza and Marek Grzes 24

Multi-Element Long Distance Dependencies: Using SPk Languages to Explore the Characteristics of Long-Distance Dependencies
Abhijit Mahalunkar and John Kelleher 34

LSTM Networks Can Perform Dynamic Counting
Mirac Suzgun, Yonatan Belinkov, Stuart Shieber and Sebastian Gehrmann 44

Conference Program

Friday, August, 2nd 2019

9:00-9:05	**Opening Remarks**
9:05-9:45	**Invited Talk:** *Do Simpler Automata Learn Better?* Kevin Knight
9:45-9:51	**Poster Spotlights:** *Sequential Neural Networks as Automata* William Merrill *Grammatical Sequence Prediction for Real-Time Neural Semantic Parsing* Chunyang Xiao, Christoph Teichmann and Konstantine Arkoudas *Siamese recurrent networks can learn first-order logic reasoning and exhibit zero-shot generalization* Mathijs Mul and Willem Zuidema
9:51-10:30	**Invited Talk:** *A story about weighted automata (WFAs), RNNs and low-rank Hankel Matrices* Ariadna Quattoni
10:30-11:00	**Break**
11:00-11:40	**Invited Talk:** *Distilling computational models from Recurrent Neural Networks* Remi Eyraud
11:40-11:45	**Poster Spotlights:** *CYK Parsing over Distributed Representations* Fabio Massimo Zanzotto, Giordano Cristini and Giorgio Satta *Relating RNN layers with the spectral WFA ranks in sequence modelling* Farhana Ferdousi Liza and Marek Grzes
11:45-12:25	**Invited Talk:** *Using formal grammars to test ability of recurrent neural networks to model long-distance dependencies in sequential data* John Kelleher
12:25-13:30	**Poster Spotlights:** *Using SPk Languages to Explore the Characteristics of Long-Distance Dependencies* Abhijit Mahalunkar and John Kelleher *LSTM Networks Can Perform Dynamic Counting* Mirac Suzgun, Yonatan Belinkov, Stuart Shieber and Sebastian Gehrmann
12:30-14:00	**Lunch**
14:00-15:30	**Poster Session**
15:30-16:00	**Break**
16:00-16:40	**Invited Talk:** *Beyond testing and acceptance: On the study of formal and natural languages in neural networks* Robert Frank
16:40-17:20	**Invited Talk:** *Rational Recurrences for Empirical Natural Language Processing* Noah Smith
17:20-17:30	**Closing Discussion**

Sequential Neural Networks as Automata

William Merrill[*]
Yale University, New Haven, CT, USA
Allen Institute for Artificial Intelligence, Seattle, WA, USA
william.merrill@yale.edu

Abstract

This work attempts to explain the types of computation that neural networks can perform by relating them to automata. We first define what it means for a real-time network with bounded precision to accept a language. A measure of network memory follows from this definition. We then characterize the classes of languages acceptable by various recurrent networks, attention, and convolutional networks. We find that LSTMs function like counter machines and relate convolutional networks to the subregular hierarchy. Overall, this work attempts to increase our understanding and ability to interpret neural networks through the lens of theory. These theoretical insights help explain neural computation, as well as the relationship between neural networks and natural language grammar.

1 Introduction

In recent years, neural networks have achieved tremendous success on a variety of natural language processing (NLP) tasks. Neural networks employ continuous distributed representations of linguistic data, which contrast with classical discrete methods. While neural methods work well, one of the downsides of the distributed representations that they utilize is interpretability. It is hard to tell what kinds of computation a model is capable of, and when a model is working, it is hard to tell what it is doing.

This work aims to address such issues of interpretability by relating sequential neural networks to forms of computation that are more well understood. In theoretical computer science, the computational capacities of many different kinds of automata formalisms are clearly established. Moreover, the Chomsky hierarchy links natural language to such automata-theoretic languages (Chomsky, 1956). Thus, relating neural networks to automata both yields insight into what general forms of computation such models can perform, as well as how such computation relates to natural language grammar.

Recent work has begun to investigate what kinds of automata-theoretic computations various types of neural networks can simulate. Weiss et al. (2018) propose a connection between long short-term memory networks (LSTMs) and counter automata. They provide a construction by which the LSTM can simulate a simplified variant of a counter automaton. They also demonstrate that LSTMs can learn to increment and decrement their cell state as counters in practice. Peng et al. (2018), on the other hand, describe a connection between the gating mechanisms of several recurrent neural network (RNN) architectures and weighted finite-state acceptors.

This paper follows Weiss et al. (2018) by analyzing the expressiveness of neural network acceptors under asymptotic conditions. We formalize asymptotic language acceptance, as well as an associated notion of network memory. We use this theory to derive computation upper bounds and automata-theoretic characterizations for several different kinds of recurrent neural networks (Section 3), as well as other architectural variants like attention (Section 4) and convolutional networks (CNNs) (Section 5). This leads to a fairly complete automata-theoretic characterization of sequential neural networks.

In Section 6, we report empirical results investigating how well these asymptotic predictions describe networks with continuous activations learned by gradient descent. In some cases, networks behave according to the theoretical predictions, but we also find cases where there is gap between the asymptotic characterization and ac-

[*] Work completed while the author was at Yale University.

Proceedings of the Workshop on Deep Learning and Formal Languages: Building Bridges, pages 1–13
Florence, Italy, August, 2nd 2019.

tual network behavior.

Still, discretizing neural networks using an asymptotic analysis builds intuition about how the network computes. Thus, this work provides insight about the types of computations that sequential neural networks can perform through the lens of formal language theory. In so doing, we can also compare the notions of grammar expressible by neural networks to formal models that have been proposed for natural language grammar.

2 Introducing the Asymptotic Analysis

To investigate the capacities of different neural network architectures, we need to first define what it means for a neural network to accept a language. There are a variety of ways to formalize language acceptance, and changes to this definition lead to dramatically different characterizations.

In their analysis of RNN expressiveness, Siegelmann and Sontag (1992) allow RNNs to perform an unbounded number of recurrent steps even after the input has been consumed. Furthermore, they assume that the hidden units of the network can have arbitrarily fine-grained precision. Under this very general definition of language acceptance, Siegelmann and Sontag (1992) found that even a simple recurrent network (SRN) can simulate a Turing machine.

We want to impose the following constraints on neural network computation, which are more realistic to how networks are trained in practice (Weiss et al., 2018):

1. *Real-time*: The network performs one iteration of computation per input symbol.
2. *Bounded precision*: The value of each cell in the network is representable by $O(\log n)$ bits on sequences of length n.

Informally, a *neural sequence acceptor* is a network which reads a variable-length sequence of characters and returns the probability that the input sequence is a valid sentence in some formal language. More precisely, we can write:

Definition 2.1 (Neural sequence acceptor). Let $\mathbf{X}$ be a matrix representation of a sentence where each row is a one-hot vector over an alphabet Σ. A neural sequence acceptor $\hat{\mathbb{1}}$ is a family of functions parameterized by weights θ. For each θ and $\mathbf{X}$, the function $\hat{\mathbb{1}}^\theta$ takes the form

$$\hat{\mathbb{1}}^\theta : \mathbf{X} \mapsto p \in (0, 1).$$

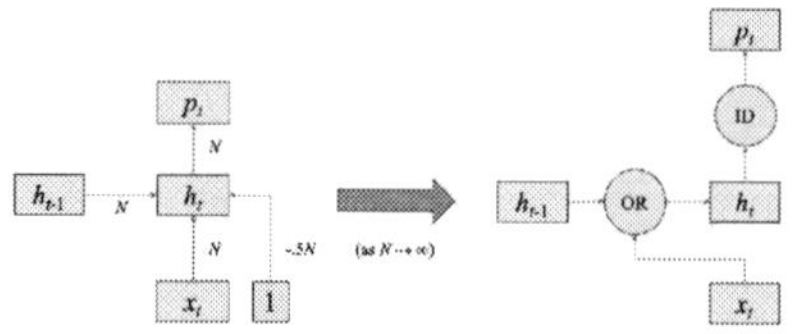

Figure 1: With sigmoid activations, the network on the left accepts a sequence of bits if and only if $x_t = 1$ for some t. On the right is the discrete computation graph that the network approaches asymptotically.

In this definition, $\hat{\mathbb{1}}$ corresponds to a general architecture like an LSTM, whereas $\hat{\mathbb{1}}^\theta$ represents a specific network, such as an LSTM with weights that have been learned from data.

In order to get an acceptance decision from this kind of network, we will consider what happens as the magnitude of its parameters gets very large. Under these asymptotic conditions, the internal connections of the network approach a discrete computation graph, and the probabilistic output approaches the indicator function of some language (Figure 1).

Definition 2.2 (Asymptotic acceptance). Let L be a language with indicator function $\mathbb{1}_L$. A neural sequence acceptor $\hat{\mathbb{1}}$ with weights θ asymptotically accepts L if

$$\lim_{N \to \infty} \hat{\mathbb{1}}^{N\theta} = \mathbb{1}_L.$$

Note that the limit of $\hat{\mathbb{1}}^{N\theta}$ represents the function that $\hat{\mathbb{1}}^{N\theta}$ converges to pointwise.[1]

Discretizing the network in this way lets us analyze it as an automaton. We can also view this discretization as a way of bounding the precision that each unit in the network can encode, since it is forced to act as a discrete unit instead of a continuous value. This prevents complex fractal representations that rely on infinite precision. We will see later that, for every architecture considered, this definition ensures that the value of every unit in the network is representable in $O(\log n)$ bits on sequences of length n.

It is important to note that real neural networks can learn strategies not allowed by the asymptotic definition. Thus, this way of analyzing neural networks is not completely faithful to their practical

[1]https://en.wikipedia.org/wiki/Pointwise_convergence

usage. In Section 6, we discuss empirical studies investigating how trained networks compare to the asymptotic predictions. While we find evidence of networks learning behavior that is not asymptotically stable, adding noise to the network during training seems to make it more difficult for the network to learn non-asymptotic strategies.

Consider a neural network that asymptotically accepts some language. For any given length, we can pick weights for the network such that it will correctly decide strings shorter than that length (Theorem A.1).

Analyzing a network's asymptotic behavior also gives us a notion of the network's memory. Weiss et al. (2018) illustrate how the LSTM's additive cell update gives it more effective memory than the squashed state of an SRN or GRU for solving counting tasks. We generalize this concept of memory capacity as *state complexity*. Informally, the state complexity of a node within a network represents the number of values that the node can achieve asymptotically as a function of the sequence length n. For example, the LSTM cell state will have $O(n^k)$ state complexity (Theorem 3.3), whereas the state of other recurrent networks has $O(1)$ (Theorem 3.1).

State complexity applies to a *hidden state* sequence, which we can define as follows:

Definition 2.3 (Hidden state)**.** For any sentence $\mathbf{X}$, let n be the length of $\mathbf{X}$. For $1 \leq t \leq n$, the k-length hidden state $\mathbf{h}_t$ with respect to parameters θ is a sequence of functions given by

$$\mathbf{h}_t^\theta : \mathbf{X} \mapsto \mathbf{v}_t \in \mathbb{R}^k.$$

Often, a sequence acceptor can be written as a function of an intermediate hidden state. For example, the output of the recurrent layer acts as a hidden state in an LSTM language acceptor. In recurrent architectures, the value of the hidden state is a function of the preceding prefix of characters, but with convolution or attention, it can depend on characters occurring after index t.

The *state complexity* is defined as the cardinality of the *configuration set* of such a hidden state:

Definition 2.4 (Configuration set)**.** For all n, the configuration set of hidden state $\mathbf{h}_n$ with respect to parameters θ is given by

$$M(\mathbf{h}_n^\theta) = \left\{ \lim_{N \to \infty} \mathbf{h}_n^{N\theta}(\mathbf{X}) \mid n = |\mathbf{X}| \right\}.$$

where $|\mathbf{X}|$ is the length, or height, of the sentence matrix $\mathbf{X}$.

Definition 2.5 (Fixed state complexity)**.** For all n, the fixed state complexity of hidden state $\mathbf{h}_n$ with respect to parameters θ is given by

$$\bowtie(\mathbf{h}_n^\theta) = \left| M(\mathbf{h}_n^\theta) \right|.$$

Definition 2.6 (General state complexity)**.** For all n, the general state complexity of hidden state $\mathbf{h}_n$ is given by

$$\bowtie(\mathbf{h}_n) = \max_\theta \bowtie(\mathbf{h}_n^\theta).$$

To illustrate these definitions, consider a simplified recurrent mechanism based on the LSTM cell. The architecture is parameterized by a vector $\theta \in \mathbb{R}^2$. At each time step, the network reads a bit x_t and computes

$$f_t = \sigma(\theta_1 x_t) \tag{1}$$

$$i_t = \sigma(\theta_2 x_t) \tag{2}$$

$$h_t = f_t h_{t-1} + i_t. \tag{3}$$

When we set $\theta^+ = \langle 1, 1 \rangle$, h_t asymptotically computes the sum of the preceding inputs. Because this sum can evaluate to any integer between 0 and n, $h_n^{\theta^+}$ has a fixed state complexity of

$$\bowtie\left(h_n^{\theta^+}\right) = O(n). \tag{4}$$

However, when we use parameters $\theta^{\mathrm{Id}} = \langle -1, 1 \rangle$, we get a reduced network where $h_t = x_t$ asymptotically. Thus,

$$\bowtie\left(h_n^{\theta^{\mathrm{Id}}}\right) = O(1). \tag{5}$$

Finally, the general state complexity is the maximum fixed complexity, which is $O(n)$.

For any neural network hidden state, the state complexity is at most $2^{O(n)}$ (Theorem A.2). This means that the value of the hidden unit can be encoded in $O(n)$ bits. Moreover, for every specific architecture considered, we observe that each fixed-length state vector has at most $O(n^k)$ state complexity, or, equivalently, can be represented in $O(\log n)$ bits.

Architectures that have exponential state complexity, such as the transformer, do so by using a variable-length hidden state. State complexity generalizes naturally to a variable-length hidden state, with the only difference being that $\mathbf{h}_t$ (Definition 2.3) becomes a sequence of variably sized objects rather than a sequence of fixed-length vectors.

Now, we consider what classes of languages different neural networks can accept asymptotically. We also analyze different architectures in terms of state complexity. The theory that emerges from these tools enables better understanding of the computational processes underlying neural sequence models.

3 Recurrent Neural Networks

As previously mentioned, RNNs are Turing-complete under an unconstrained definition of acceptance (Siegelmann and Sontag, 1992). The classical reduction of a Turing machine to an RNN relies on two unrealistic assumptions about RNN computation (Weiss et al., 2018). First, the number of recurrent computations must be unbounded in the length of the input, whereas, in practice, RNNs are almost always trained in a real-time fashion. Second, it relies heavily on infinite precision of the network's logits. We will see that the asymptotic analysis, which restricts computation to be real-time and have bounded precision, severely narrows the class of formal languages that an RNN can accept.

3.1 Simple Recurrent Networks

The SRN, or Elman network, is the simplest type of RNN (Elman, 1990):

Definition 3.1 (SRN layer).

$$\mathbf{h}_t = \tanh(\mathbf{W}\mathbf{x}_t + \mathbf{U}\mathbf{h}_{t-1} + \mathbf{b}). \quad (6)$$

A well-known problem with SRNs is that they struggle with long-distance dependencies. One explanation of this is the vanishing gradient problem, which motivated the development of more sophisticated architectures like the LSTM (Hochreiter and Schmidhuber, 1997). Another shortcoming of the SRN is that, in some sense, it has less memory than the LSTM. This is because, while both architectures have a fixed number of hidden units, the SRN units remain between -1 and 1, whereas the value of each LSTM cell can grow unboundedly (Weiss et al., 2018). We can formalize this intuition by showing that the SRN has finite state complexity:

Theorem 3.1 (SRN state complexity). *For any length n, the SRN cell state $\mathbf{h}_n \in \mathbb{R}^k$ has state complexity*

$$\mathsf{M}(\mathbf{h}_n) \leq 2^k = O(1).$$

Proof. For every n, each unit of $\mathbf{h}_n$ will be the output of a $\tanh$. In the limit, it can achieve either -1 or 1. Thus, for the full vector, the number of configurations is bounded by 2^k. □

It also follows from Theorem 3.1 that the languages asymptotically acceptable by an SRN are a subset of the finite-state (i.e. regular) languages. Lemma B.1 provides the other direction of this containment. Thus, SRNs are equivalent to finite-state automata.

Theorem 3.2 (SRN characterization). *Let $L(\mathrm{SRN})$ denote the languages acceptable by an SRN, and* RL *the regular languages. Then,*

$$L(\mathrm{SRN}) = \mathrm{RL}.$$

This characterization is quite diminished compared to Turing completeness. It is also more descriptive of what SRNs can express in practice. We will see that LSTMs, on the other hand, are strictly more powerful than the regular languages.

3.2 Long Short-Term Memory Networks

An LSTM is a recurrent network with a complex gating mechanism that determines how information from one time step is passed to the next. Originally, this gating mechanism was designed to remedy the vanishing gradient problem in SRNs, or, equivalently, to make it easier for the network to remember long-term dependencies (Hochreiter and Schmidhuber, 1997). Due to strong empirical performance on many language tasks, LSTMs have become a canonical model for NLP.

Weiss et al. (2018) suggest that another advantage of the LSTM architecture is that it can use its cell state as counter memory. They point out that this constitutes a real difference between the LSTM and the GRU, whose update equations do not allow it to increment or decrement its memory units. We will further investigate this connection between LSTMs and counter machines.

Definition 3.2 (LSTM layer).

$$\mathbf{f}_t = \sigma(\mathbf{W}^f\mathbf{x}_t + \mathbf{U}^f\mathbf{h}_{t-1} + \mathbf{b}^f) \quad (7)$$
$$\mathbf{i}_t = \sigma(\mathbf{W}^i\mathbf{x}_t + \mathbf{U}^i\mathbf{h}_{t-1} + \mathbf{b}^i) \quad (8)$$
$$\mathbf{o}_t = \sigma(\mathbf{W}^o\mathbf{x}_t + \mathbf{U}^o\mathbf{h}_{t-1} + \mathbf{b}^o) \quad (9)$$
$$\tilde{\mathbf{c}}_t = \tanh(\mathbf{W}^c\mathbf{x}_t + \mathbf{U}^c\mathbf{h}_{t-1} + \mathbf{b}^c) \quad (10)$$
$$\mathbf{c}_t = \mathbf{f}_t \odot \mathbf{c}_{t-1} + \mathbf{i}_t \odot \tilde{\mathbf{c}}_t \quad (11)$$
$$\mathbf{h}_t = \mathbf{o}_t \odot f(\mathbf{c}_t). \quad (12)$$

In (12), we set f to either the identity or $\tanh$ (Weiss et al., 2018), although $\tanh$ is more standard in practice. The vector $\mathbf{h}_t$ is the output that is received by the next layer, and $\mathbf{c}_t$ is an unexposed memory vector called the cell state.

Theorem 3.3 (LSTM state complexity). *The LSTM cell state $\mathbf{c}_n \in \mathbb{R}^k$ has state complexity*

$$\mathsf{M}(\mathbf{c}_n) = O(n^k).$$

Proof. At each time step t, we know that the configuration sets of $\mathbf{f}_t$, $\mathbf{i}_t$, and $\mathbf{o}_t$ are each subsets of $\{0,1\}^k$. Similarly, the configuration set of $\tilde{\mathbf{c}}_t$ is a subset of $\{-1,1\}^k$. This allows us to rewrite the elementwise recurrent update as

$$\lim_{N\to\infty} [\mathbf{c}_t]_i = \lim_{N\to\infty} [\mathbf{f}_t]_i[\mathbf{c}_{t-1}]_i + [\mathbf{i}_t]_i[\tilde{\mathbf{c}}_t]_i \quad (13)$$

$$= \lim_{N\to\infty} a[\mathbf{c}_{t-1}]_i + b \quad (14)$$

where $a \in \{0,1\}$ and $b \in \{-1,0,1\}$.

Let S_t be the configuration set of $[\mathbf{c}_t]_i$. At each time step, we have exactly two ways to produce a new value in S_t that was not in S_{t-1}: either we decrement the minimum value in S_{t-1} or increment the maximum value. It follows that

$$|S_t| = 2 + |S_{t-1}| \quad (15)$$

$$\implies |S_n| = O(n). \quad (16)$$

For all k units of the cell state, we get

$$\mathsf{M}(\mathbf{c}_n) \le |S_n|^k = O(n^k). \quad (17)$$

□

The construction in Theorem 3.3 produces a counter machine whose counter and state update functions are linearly separable. Thus, we have an upper bound on the expressive power of the LSTM:

Theorem 3.4 (LSTM upper bound). *Let* CL *be the real-time counter languages (Fischer, 1966; Fischer et al., 1968). Then,*

$$L(\mathrm{LSTM}) \subseteq \mathrm{CL}.$$

Theorem 3.4 constitutes a very tight upper bound on the expressiveness of LSTM computation. Asymptotically, LSTMs are not powerful enough to model even the deterministic context-free language $w\#w^R$.

Weiss et al. (2018) show how the LSTM can simulate a simplified variant of the counter machine. Combining these results, we see that the asymptotic expressiveness of the LSTM falls somewhere between the general and simplified counter languages. This suggests counting is a good way to understand the behavior of LSTMs.

3.3 Gated Recurrent Units

The GRU is a popular gated recurrent architecture that is in many ways similar to the LSTM (Cho et al., 2014). Rather than having separate forget and input gates, the GRU utilizes a single gate that controls both functions.

Definition 3.3 (GRU layer).

$$\mathbf{z}_t = \sigma(\mathbf{W}^z\mathbf{x}_t + \mathbf{U}^z\mathbf{h}_{t-1} + \mathbf{b}^z) \quad (18)$$

$$\mathbf{r}_t = \sigma(\mathbf{W}^r\mathbf{x}_t + \mathbf{U}^r\mathbf{h}_{t-1} + \mathbf{b}^r) \quad (19)$$

$$\mathbf{u}_t = \tanh\left(\mathbf{W}^u\mathbf{x}_t + \mathbf{U}^u(\mathbf{r}_t \odot \mathbf{h}_{t-1}) + \mathbf{b}^u\right) \quad (20)$$

$$\mathbf{h}_t = \mathbf{z}_t \odot \mathbf{h}_{t-1} + (1 - \mathbf{z}_t) \odot \mathbf{u}_t. \quad (21)$$

Weiss et al. (2018) observe that GRUs do not exhibit the same counter behavior as LSTMs on languages like a^nb^n. As with the SRN, the GRU state is squashed between -1 and 1 (20). Taken together, Lemmas C.1 and C.2 show that GRUs, like SRNs, are finite-state.

Theorem 3.5 (GRU characterization).

$$L(\mathrm{GRU}) = \mathrm{RL}.$$

3.4 RNN Complexity Hierarchy

Synthesizing all of these results, we get the following complexity hierarchy:

$$\mathrm{RL} = L(\mathrm{SRN}) = L(\mathrm{GRU}) \quad (22)$$

$$\subset \mathrm{SCL} \subseteq L(\mathrm{LSTM}) \subseteq \mathrm{CL}. \quad (23)$$

Basic recurrent architectures have finite state, whereas the LSTM is strictly more powerful than a finite-state machine.

4 Attention

Attention is a popular enhancement to sequence-to-sequence (seq2seq) neural networks (Bahdanau et al., 2014; Chorowski et al., 2015; Luong et al., 2015). Attention allows a network to recall specific encoder states while trying to produce output. In the context of machine translation, this mechanism models the alignment between words in the source and target languages. More recent work has found that "attention is all you need" (Vaswani et al., 2017; Radford et al., 2018). In other words, networks with only attention and no recurrent connections perform at the state of the art on many tasks.

An attention function maps a query vector and a sequence of paired key-value vectors to a weighted combination of the values. This lookup function is meant to retrieve the values whose keys resemble the query.

Definition 4.1 (Dot-product attention). For any n, define a query vector $\mathbf{q} \in \mathbb{R}^l$, matrix of key vectors $\mathbf{K} \in \mathbb{R}^{nl}$, and matrix of value vectors $\mathbf{V} \in \mathbb{R}^{nk}$. Dot-product attention is given by

$$\mathrm{attn}(\mathbf{q}, \mathbf{K}, \mathbf{V}) = \mathrm{softmax}(\mathbf{q}\mathbf{K}^T)\mathbf{V}.$$

In Definition 4.1, softmax creates a vector of similarity scores between the query $\mathbf{q}$ and the key vectors in $\mathbf{K}$. The output of attention is thus a weighted sum of the value vectors where the weight for each value represents its relevance.

In practice, the dot product $\mathbf{q}\mathbf{K}^T$ is often scaled by the square root of the length of the query vector (Vaswani et al., 2017). However, this is only done to improve optimization and has no effect on expressiveness. Therefore, we consider the unscaled version.

In the asymptotic case, attention reduces to a weighted average of the values whose keys maximally resemble the query. This can be viewed as an $\arg\max$ operation.

Theorem 4.1 (Asymptotic attention). *Let $t_1, .., t_m$ be the subsequence of time steps that maximize $\mathbf{q}\mathbf{k}_t$.*[2] *Asymptotically, attention computes*

$$\lim_{N\to\infty} \mathrm{attn}\left(\mathbf{q}, \mathbf{K}, \mathbf{V}\right) = \lim_{N\to\infty} \frac{1}{m} \sum_{i=1}^{m} \mathbf{v}_{t_i}.$$

Corollary 4.1.1 (Asymptotic attention with unique maximum). *If $\mathbf{q}\mathbf{k}_t$ has a unique maximum over $1 \leq t \leq n$, then attention asymptotically computes*

$$\lim_{N\to\infty} \mathrm{attn}\left(\mathbf{q}, \mathbf{K}, \mathbf{V}\right) = \lim_{N\to\infty} \arg\max_{\mathbf{v}_t} \mathbf{q}\mathbf{k}_t.$$

Now, we analyze the effect of adding attention to an acceptor network. Because we are concerned with language acceptance instead of transduction, we consider a simplified seq2seq attention model where the output sequence has length 1:

Definition 4.2 (Attention layer). Let the hidden state $\mathbf{v}_1, .., \mathbf{v}_n$ be the output of an encoder network where the union of the asymptotic configuration sets over all $\mathbf{v}_t$ is finite. We attend over $\mathbf{V}_t$, the matrix stacking $\mathbf{v}_1, .., \mathbf{v}_t$, by computing

$$\mathbf{h}_t = \mathrm{attn}(\mathbf{W}^q\mathbf{v}_t, \mathbf{V}_t, \mathbf{V}_t).$$

In this model, $\mathbf{h}_t$ represents a summary of the relevant information in the prefix $\mathbf{v}_1, .., \mathbf{v}_t$. The query that is used to attend at time t is a simple linear transformation of $\mathbf{v}_t$.

In addition to modeling alignment, attention improves a bounded-state model by providing additional memory. By converting the state of the network to a growing sequence $\mathbf{V}_t$ instead of a fixed length vector $\mathbf{v}_t$, attention enables $2^{\Theta(n)}$ state complexity.

Theorem 4.2 (Encoder state complexity). *The full state of the attention layer has state complexity*

$$\bowtie(\mathbf{V}_n) = 2^{\Theta(n)}.$$

The $O(n^k)$ complexity of the LSTM architecture means that it is impossible for LSTMs to copy or reverse long strings. The exponential state complexity provided by attention enables copying, which we can view as a simplified version of machine translation. Thus, it makes sense that attention is almost universal in machine translation architectures. The additional memory introduced by attention might also allow more complex hierarchical representations.

A natural follow-up question to Theorem 4.2 is whether this additional complexity is preserved in the attention summary vector $\mathbf{h}_n$. Attending over $\mathbf{V}_n$ does not preserve exponential state complexity. Instead, we get an $O(n^2)$ summary of $\mathbf{V}_n$.

Theorem 4.3 (Summary state complexity). *The attention summary vector has state complexity*

$$\bowtie(\mathbf{h}_n) = O(n^2).$$

With minimal additional assumptions, we can show a more restrictive bound: namely, that the complexity of the summary vector is finite. Appendix D discusses this in more detail.

5 Convolutional Networks

While CNNs were originally developed for image processing (Krizhevsky et al., 2012), they are also

[2]To be precise, we can define a maximum over the similarity scores according to the order given by

$$f > g \iff \lim_{N\to\infty} f(N) - g(N) > 0. \quad (24)$$

used to encode sequences. One popular application of this is to build character-level representations of words (Kim et al., 2016). Another example is the capsule network architecture of Zhao et al. (2018), which uses a convolutional layer as an initial feature extractor over a sentence.

Definition 5.1 (CNN acceptor).

$$\mathbf{h}_t = \tanh\left(\mathbf{W}^h(\mathbf{x}_{t-k}\|..\|\mathbf{x}_{t+k}) + \mathbf{b}^h\right) \quad (25)$$

$$\mathbf{h}_+ = \mathrm{maxpool}(\mathbf{H}) \quad (26)$$

$$p = \sigma(\mathbf{W}^a\mathbf{h}_+ + \mathbf{b}^a). \quad (27)$$

In this network, the k-convolutional layer (25) produces a vector-valued sequence of outputs. This sequence is then collapsed to a fixed length by taking the maximum value of each filter over all the time steps (26).

The CNN acceptor is much weaker than the LSTM. Since the vector $\mathbf{h}_t$ has finite state, we see that $L(\mathrm{CNN}) \subseteq \mathrm{RL}$. Moreover, simple regular languages like a^*ba^* are beyond the CNN (Lemma E.1). Thus, the subset relation is strict.

Theorem 5.1 (CNN upper bound).

$$L(\mathrm{CNN}) \subset \mathrm{RL}.$$

So, to arrive at a characterization of CNNs, we should move to subregular languages. In particular, we consider the strictly local languages (Rogers and Pullum, 2011).

Theorem 5.2 (CNN lower bound). *Let* SL *be the strictly local languages. Then,*

$$\mathrm{SL} \subseteq L(\mathrm{CNN}).$$

Notably, strictly local formalisms have been proposed as a computational model for phonological grammar (Heinz et al., 2011). We might take this to explain why CNNs have been successful at modeling character-level information.

However, Heinz et al. (2011) suggest that a generalization to the tier-based strictly local languages is necessary to account for the full range of phonological phenomena. Tier-based strictly local grammars can target characters in a specific tier of the vocabulary (e.g. vowels) instead of applying to the full string. While a single convolutional layer cannot utilize tiers, it is conceivable that a more complex architecture with recurrent connections could.

6 Empirical Results

In this section, we compare our theoretical characterizations for asymptotic networks to the empirical performance of trained neural networks with continuous logits.[3]

6.1 Counting

The goal of this experiment is to evaluate which architectures have memory beyond finite state. We train a language model on a^nb^nc with $5 \leq n \leq 1000$ and test it on longer strings ($2000 \leq n \leq 2200$). Predicting the c character correctly while maintaining good overall accuracy requires $O(n)$ states. The results reported in Table 1 demonstrate that all recurrent models, with only two hidden units, find a solution to this task that generalizes at least over this range of string lengths.

Weiss et al. (2018) report failures in attempts to train SRNs and GRUs to accept counter languages, unlike what we have found. We conjecture that this stems not from the requisite memory, but instead from the different objective function we used. Our language modeling training objective is a robust and transferable learning target (Radford et al., 2019), whereas sparse acceptance classification might be challenging to learn directly for long strings.

Weiss et al. (2018) also observe that LSTMs use their memory as counters in a straightforwardly interpretable manner, whereas SRNs and GRUs do not do so in any obvious way. Despite this, our results show that SRNs and GRUs are nonetheless able to implement generalizable counter memory while processing strings of significant length. Because the strategies learned by these architectures are not asymptotically stable, however, their schemes for encoding counting are less interpretable.

6.2 Counting with Noise

In order to abstract away from asymptotically unstable representations, our next experiment investigates how adding noise to an RNN's activations impacts its ability to count. For the SRN and GRU, noise is added to $\mathbf{h}_{t-1}$ before computing $\mathbf{h}_t$, and for the LSTM, noise is added to $\mathbf{c}_{t-1}$. In either case, the noise is sampled from the distribution $N(0, 0.1^2)$.

[3] https://github.com/viking-sudo-rm/nn-automata

		No Noise		Noise	
	$\mathbb{M}$	Acc	Acc on c	Acc	Acc on c
SRN	$O(1)$	100.0	100.0	49.9	100.0
GRU	$O(1)$	99.9	100.0	53.9	100.0
LSTM	$O(n^k)$	99.9	100.0	99.9	100.0

Table 1: Generalization performance of language models trained on $a^n b^n c$. Each model has 2 hidden units.

	$\mathbb{M}$	Val Acc	Gen Acc
LSTM	$O(n^k)$	94.0	51.6
LSTM-Attn	$2^{\Theta(n)}$	100.0	51.7
LSTM	$O(n^k)$	92.5	73.3
StackNN	$2^{\Theta(n)}$	100.0	100.0

Table 2: Max validation and generalization accuracies on string reversal over 10 trials. The top section shows our seq2seq LSTM with and without attention. The bottom reports the LSTM and StackNN results of Hao et al. (2018). Each LSTM has 10 hidden units.

The results reported in the right column of Table 1 show that the noisy SRN and GRU now fail to count, whereas the noisy LSTM remains successful. Thus, the asymptotic characterization of each architecture matches the capacity of a trained network when a small amount of noise is introduced.

From a practical perspective, training neural networks with Gaussian noise is one way of improving generalization by preventing overfitting (Bishop, 1995; Noh et al., 2017). From this point of view, asymptotic characterizations might be more descriptive of the generalization capacities of regularized neural networks of the sort necessary to learn the patterns in natural language data as opposed to the unregularized networks that are typically used to learn the patterns in carefully curated formal languages.

6.3 Reversing

Another important formal language task for assessing network memory is string reversal. Reversing requires remembering a $\Theta(n)$ prefix of characters, which implies $2^{\Theta(n)}$ state complexity.

We frame reversing as a seq2seq transduction task, and compare the performance of an LSTM encoder-decoder architecture to the same architecture augmented with attention. We also report the results of Hao et al. (2018) for a stack neural network (StackNN), another architecture with $2^{\Theta(n)}$ state complexity (Lemma F.1).

Following Hao et al. (2018), the models were trained on 800 random binary strings with length $\sim N(10, 2)$ and evaluated on strings with length $\sim N(50, 5)$. As can be seen in Table 2, the LSTM with attention achieves 100.0% validation accuracy, but fails to generalize to longer strings. In contrast, Hao et al. (2018) report that a stack neural network can learn and generalize string reversal flawlessly. In both cases, it seems that having $2^{\Theta(n)}$ state complexity enables better performance on this memory-demanding task. However, our seq2seq LSTMs appear to be biased against finding a strategy that generalizes to longer strings.

7 Conclusion

We have introduced asymptotic acceptance as a new way to characterize neural networks as automata of different sorts. It provides a useful and generalizable tool for building intuition about how a network works, as well as for comparing the formal properties of different architectures. Further, by combining asymptotic characterizations with existing results in mathematical linguistics, we can better assess the suitability of different architectures for the representation of natural language grammar.

We observe empirically, however, that this discrete analysis fails to fully characterize the range of behaviors expressible by neural networks. In particular, RNNs predicted to be finite-state solve a task that requires more than finite memory. On the other hand, introducing a small amount of noise into a network's activations seems to prevent it from implementing non-asymptotic strategies. Thus, asymptotic characterizations might be a good model for the types of generalizable strategies that noise-regularized neural networks trained on natural language data can learn.

Acknowledgements

Thank you to Dana Angluin and Robert Frank for their insightful advice and support on this project.

References

Dzmitry Bahdanau, Kyunghyun Cho, and Yoshua Bengio. 2014. Neural machine translation by jointly learning to align and translate. *arXiv preprint arXiv:1409.0473.*

Chris M. Bishop. 1995. Training with noise is equivalent to Tikhonov regularization. *Neural Comput.*, 7(1):108–116.

Kyunghyun Cho, Bart van Merrienboer, Caglar Gulcehre, Dzmitry Bahdanau, Fethi Bougares, Holger Schwenk, and Yoshua Bengio. 2014. Learning phrase representations using RNN encoder–decoder for statistical machine translation. In *Proceedings of the 2014 Conference on Empirical Methods in Natural Language Processing (EMNLP)*, pages 1724–1734, Doha, Qatar. Association for Computational Linguistics.

Noam Chomsky. 1956. Three models for the description of language. *IRE Transactions on information theory*, 2(3):113–124.

Jan K Chorowski, Dzmitry Bahdanau, Dmitriy Serdyuk, Kyunghyun Cho, and Yoshua Bengio. 2015. Attention-based models for speech recognition. In *Advances in neural information processing systems*, pages 577–585.

Jeffrey L Elman. 1990. Finding structure in time. *Cognitive science*, 14(2):179–211.

Patrick C Fischer. 1966. Turing machines with restricted memory access. *Information and Control*, 9(4):364–379.

Patrick C. Fischer, Albert R. Meyer, and Arnold L. Rosenberg. 1968. Counter machines and counter languages. *Mathematical systems theory*, 2(3):265–283.

Yiding Hao, William Merrill, Dana Angluin, Robert Frank, Noah Amsel, Andrew Benz, and Simon Mendelsohn. 2018. Context-free transductions with neural stacks. *arXiv preprint arXiv:1809.02836.*

Jeffrey Heinz, Chetan Rawal, and Herbert G Tanner. 2011. Tier-based strictly local constraints for phonology. In *Proceedings of the 49th Annual Meeting of the Association for Computational Linguistics: Human Language Technologies: short papers-Volume 2*, pages 58–64. Association for Computational Linguistics.

Sepp Hochreiter and Jürgen Schmidhuber. 1997. Long short-term memory. *Neural computation*, 9(8):1735–1780.

Yoon Kim, Yacine Jernite, David Sontag, and Alexander M Rush. 2016. Character-aware neural language models. In *AAAI*, pages 2741–2749.

Alex Krizhevsky, Ilya Sutskever, and Geoffrey E Hinton. 2012. Imagenet classification with deep convolutional neural networks. In *Advances in neural information processing systems*, pages 1097–1105.

Minh-Thang Luong, Hieu Pham, and Christopher D Manning. 2015. Effective approaches to attention-based neural machine translation. *arXiv preprint arXiv:1508.04025.*

Hyeonwoo Noh, Tackgeun You, Jonghwan Mun, and Bohyung Han. 2017. Regularizing deep neural networks by noise: Its interpretation and optimization. In *Advances in Neural Information Processing Systems 30: Annual Conference on Neural Information Processing Systems 2017, 4-9 December 2017, Long Beach, CA, USA*, pages 5115–5124.

Hao Peng, Roy Schwartz, Sam Thomson, and Noah A Smith. 2018. Rational recurrences. *arXiv preprint arXiv:1808.09357.*

Alec Radford, Karthik Narasimhan, Tim Salimans, and Ilya Sutskever. 2018. Improving language understanding by generative pre-training.

Alec Radford, Jeffrey Wu, Rewon Child, David Luan, Dario Amodei, and Ilya Sutskever. 2019. Language models are unsupervised multitask learners. *URL https://openai. com/blog/better-language-models.*

James Rogers and Geoffrey K Pullum. 2011. Aural pattern recognition experiments and the subregular hierarchy. *Journal of Logic, Language and Information*, 20(3):329–342.

Hava T. Siegelmann and Eduardo D. Sontag. 1992. On the computational power of neural nets. In *Proceedings of the Fifth Annual Workshop on Computational Learning Theory*, COLT '92, pages 440–449, New York, NY, USA. ACM.

Ashish Vaswani, Noam Shazeer, Niki Parmar, Jakob Uszkoreit, Llion Jones, Aidan N Gomez, Łukasz Kaiser, and Illia Polosukhin. 2017. Attention is all you need. In *Advances in Neural Information Processing Systems*, pages 5998–6008.

Gail Weiss, Yoav Goldberg, and Eran Yahav. 2018. On the practical computational power of finite precision RNNs for language recognition. *CoRR*, abs/1805.04908.

Wei Zhao, Jianbo Ye, Min Yang, Zeyang Lei, Suofei Zhang, and Zhou Zhao. 2018. Investigating capsule networks with dynamic routing for text classification. *arXiv preprint arXiv:1804.00538.*

A Asymptotic Acceptance and State Complexity

Theorem A.1 (Arbitary approximation). *Let $\hat{\mathbb{1}}$ be a neural sequence acceptor for L. For all m, there exist parameters θ_m such that, for any string $\mathbf{x}_1, .., \mathbf{x}_n$ with $n < m$,*

$$\left[\hat{\mathbb{1}}^{\theta_m}(\mathbf{X})\right] = \mathbb{1}_L(\mathbf{X})$$

where $[\cdot]$ rounds to the nearest integer.

Proof. Consider a string $\mathbf{X}$. By the definition of asymptotic acceptance, there exists some number $M_{\mathbf{X}}$ which is the smallest number such that, for all $N \geq M_{\mathbf{X}}$,

$$\left|\hat{\mathbb{1}}^{N\theta}(\mathbf{X}) - \mathbb{1}_L(\mathbf{X})\right| < \frac{1}{2} \tag{28}$$

$$\implies \left[\hat{\mathbb{1}}^{N\theta}(\mathbf{X})\right] = \mathbb{1}_L(\mathbf{X}). \tag{29}$$

Now, let X_m be the set of sentences $\mathbf{X}$ with length less than m. Since X_m is finite, we pick θ_m just by taking

$$\theta_m = \max_{\mathbf{X} \in X_m} M_{\mathbf{X}}\theta. \tag{30}$$

□

Theorem A.2 (General bound on state complexity). *Let $\mathbf{h}_t$ be a neural network hidden state. For any length n, it holds that*

$$\mathsf{M}(\mathbf{h}_n) = 2^{O(n)}.$$

Proof. The number of configurations of $\mathbf{h}_n$ cannot be more than the number of distinct inputs to the network. By construction, each $\mathbf{x}_t$ is a one-hot vector over the alphabet Σ. Thus, the state complexity is bounded according to

$$\mathsf{M}(\mathbf{h}_n) \leq |\Sigma|^n = 2^{O(n)}.$$

□

B SRN Lemmas

Lemma B.1 (SRN lower bound).

$$\mathrm{RL} \subseteq L(\mathrm{SRN}).$$

Proof. We must show that any language acceptable by a finite-state machine is SRN-acceptable. We need to asymptotically compute a representation of the machine's state in $\mathbf{h}_t$. We do this by storing all values of the following finite predicate at each time step:

$$\eth_t(i, \alpha) \iff q_{t-1}(i) \wedge x_t = \alpha \tag{31}$$

where $q_t(i)$ is true if the machine is in state i at time t.

Let F be the set of accepting states for the machine, and let δ^{-1} be the inverse transition relation. Assuming $\mathbf{h}_t$ asymptotically computes $\eth_t$, we can decide to accept or reject in the final layer according to the linearly separable disjunction

$$a_t \iff \bigvee_{i \in F} \bigvee_{\langle j, \alpha \rangle \in \delta^{-1}(i)} \eth_t(j, \alpha). \tag{32}$$

We now show how to recurrently compute $\eth_t$ at each time step. By rewriting q_{t-1} in terms of the previous $\eth_{t-1}$ values, we get the following recurrence:

$$\eth_t(i, \alpha) \iff x_t = \alpha \wedge \bigvee_{\langle j, \beta \rangle \in \delta^{-1}(i)} \eth_t(j, \beta). \tag{33}$$

Since this formula is linearly separable, we can compute it in a single neural network layer from $\mathbf{x}_t$ and $\mathbf{h}_{t-1}$.

Finally, we consider the base case. We need to ensure that transitions out of the initial state work out correctly at the first time step. We do this by adding a new memory unit f_t to $\mathbf{h}_t$ which is always rewritten to have value 1. Thus, if $f_{t-1} = 0$, we can be sure we are in the initial time step. For each transition out of the initial state, we add $f_{t-1} = 0$ as an additional term to get

$$\eth_t(0, \alpha) \iff x_t = \alpha \wedge \left(f_{t-1} = 0 \vee \bigvee_{\langle j, \beta \rangle \in \delta^{-1}(0)} \eth_t(j, \beta)\right). \tag{34}$$

This equation is still linearly separable and guarantees that the initial step will be computed correctly. □

C GRU Lemmas

These results follow similar arguments to those in Subsection 3.1 and Appendix B.

Lemma C.1 (GRU state complexity). *The GRU hidden state has state complexity*

$$\mathsf{M}(\mathbf{h}_n) = O(1).$$

Proof. The configuration set of $\mathbf{z}_t$ is a subset of $\{0, 1\}^k$. Thus, we have two possibilities for each value of $[\mathbf{h}_t]_i$: either $[\mathbf{h}_{t-1}]_i$ or $[\mathbf{u}_t]_i$. Furthermore, the configuration set of $[\mathbf{u}_t]_i$ is a subset of $\{-1, 1\}$. Let S_t be the configuration set of $[\mathbf{h}_t]_i$. We can describe S_t according to

$$S_0 = \{0\} \tag{35}$$

$$S_t \subseteq S_{t-1} \cup \{-1, 1\}. \tag{36}$$

This implies that, at most, there are only three possible values for each logit: -1, 0, or 1. Thus, the state complexity of $\mathbf{h}_n$ is

$$\mathsf{M}(\mathbf{h}_n) \leq 3^k = O(1). \tag{37}$$

□

Lemma C.2 (GRU lower bound)**.**

$$\mathrm{RL} \subseteq L(\mathrm{GRU}).$$

Proof. We can simulate a finite-state machine using the $\eth$ construction from Theorem 3.2. We compute values for the following predicate at each time step:

$$\eth_t(i, \alpha) \iff x_t = \alpha \wedge \bigvee_{\langle j, \beta \rangle \in \delta^{-1}(i)} \eth_{t-1}(j, \beta). \tag{38}$$

Since (38) is linearly separable, we can store $\eth_t$ in our hidden state $\mathbf{h}_t$ and recurrently compute its update. The base case can be handled similarly to (34). A final feedforward layer accepts or rejects according to (32). □

D Attention Lemmas

Theorem D.1 (Theorem 4.1 restated)**.** *Let $t_1, .., t_m$ be the subsequence of time steps that maximize $\mathbf{q}\mathbf{k}_t$. Asymptotically, attention computes*

$$\lim_{N \to \infty} \mathrm{attn}\left(\mathbf{q}, \mathbf{K}, \mathbf{V}\right) = \lim_{N \to \infty} \frac{1}{m} \sum_{i=1}^{m} \mathbf{v}_{t_i}.$$

Proof. Observe that, asymptotically, $\mathrm{softmax}(\mathbf{u})$ approaches a function

$$\lim_{N \to \infty} \mathrm{softmax}(N\mathbf{u})_t = \begin{cases} \frac{1}{m} & \text{if } u_t = \max(\mathbf{u}) \\ 0 & \text{otherwise.} \end{cases} \tag{39}$$

Thus, the output of the attention mechanism reduces to the sum

$$\lim_{N \to \infty} \sum_{i=1}^{m} \frac{1}{m} \mathbf{v}_{t_i}. \tag{40}$$

□

Lemma D.1 (Theorem 4.2 restated)**.** *The full state of the attention layer has state complexity*

$$\mathbb{M}(\mathbf{V}_n) = 2^{\Theta(n)}.$$

Proof. By the general upper bound on state complexity (Theorem A.2), we know that $\mathbb{M}(\mathbf{V}_n) = 2^{O(n)}$. We now show the lower bound.

We pick weights θ in the encoder such that $\mathbf{v}_t = \mathbf{x}_t$. Thus, $\mathbb{M}(\mathbf{v}_t^\theta) = |\Sigma|$ for all t. Since the values at each time step are independent, we know that

$$\mathbb{M}(\mathbf{V}_n^\theta) = |\Sigma|^n \tag{41}$$

$$\therefore \mathbb{M}(\mathbf{V}_n) = 2^{\Omega(n)}. \tag{42}$$

□

Lemma D.2 (Theorem 4.3 restated)**.** *The attention summary vector has state complexity*

$$\mathbb{M}(\mathbf{h}_n) = O(n^2).$$

Proof. By Theorem 4.1, we know that

$$\lim_{N \to \infty} \mathbf{h}_n = \lim_{N \to \infty} \frac{1}{m} \sum_{i=1}^{m} \mathbf{v}_{t_i}. \tag{43}$$

By construction, there is a finite set S containing all possible configurations of every $\mathbf{v}_t$. We bound the number of configurations for each $\mathbf{v}_{t_i}$ by $|S|$ to get

$$\mathbb{M}(\mathbf{h}_n) \leq \sum_{m=1}^{n} |S|m \leq |S|n^2 = O(n^2). \tag{44}$$

□

Lemma D.3 (Attention state complexity lower bound)**.** *The attention summary vector has state complexity*

$$\mathbb{M}(\mathbf{h}_n) = \Omega(n).$$

Proof. Consider the case where keys and values have dimension 1. Further, let the input strings come from a binary alphabet $\Sigma = \{0, 1\}$. We pick parameters θ in the encoder such that, for all t,

$$\lim_{N \to \infty} v_t = \begin{cases} 0 & \text{if } \mathbf{x}_t = \mathbf{0} \\ 1 & \text{otherwise} \end{cases} \tag{45}$$

and $\lim_{N \to \infty} k_t = 1$. Then, attention returns

$$\lim_{N \to \infty} \sum_{t=1}^{n} v_t = \frac{l}{n} \tag{46}$$

where l is the number of t such that $\mathbf{x}_t = \mathbf{1}$. We can vary the input to produce l from 1 to n. Thus, we have

$$\mathbb{M}(\mathbf{h}_n^\theta) = n \tag{47}$$

$$\therefore \mathbb{M}(\mathbf{h}_n) = \Omega(n). \tag{48}$$

□

Lemma D.4 (Attention state complexity with unique maximum)**.** *If, for all $\mathbf{X}$, there exists a unique t^* such that $t^* = \max_t \mathbf{q}_n \mathbf{k}_t$, then*

$$\mathbb{M}(\mathbf{h}_n) = O(1).$$

Proof. If $\mathbf{q}_n\mathbf{k}_t$ has a unique maximum, then by Corollary 4.1.1 attention returns

$$\lim_{N\to\infty} \arg\max_{\mathbf{v}_t} \mathbf{q}\mathbf{k}_t = \lim_{N\to\infty} \mathbf{v}_{t^*}. \tag{49}$$

By construction, there is a finite set S which is a superset of the configuration set of $\mathbf{v}_{t^*}$. Thus,

$$\mathcal{M}(\mathbf{h}_n) \leq |S| = O(1). \tag{50}$$

□

Lemma D.5 (Attention state complexity with ReLU activations). *If* $\lim_{N\to\infty} \mathbf{v}_t \in \{0, \infty\}^k$ *for* $1 \leq t \leq n$, *then*

$$\mathcal{M}(\mathbf{h}_n) = O(1).$$

Proof. By Theorem 4.1, we know that attention computes

$$\lim_{N\to\infty} \mathbf{h}_n = \lim_{N\to\infty} \frac{1}{m} \sum_{i=1}^{m} \mathbf{v}_{t_i}. \tag{51}$$

This sum evaluates to a vector in $\{0, \infty\}^k$, which means that

$$\mathcal{M}(\mathbf{h}_n) \leq 2^k = O(1). \tag{52}$$

□

Lemma D.5 applies if the sequence $\mathbf{v}_1, .., \mathbf{v}_n$ is computed as the output of ReLU. A similar result holds if it is computed as the output of an unsquashed linear transformation.

E CNN Lemmas

Lemma E.1 (CNN counterexample).

$$a^*ba^* \notin L(\mathrm{CNN}).$$

Proof. By contradiction. Assume we can write a network with window size k that accepts any string with exactly one b and reject any other string. Consider a string with two bs at indices i and j where $|i - j| > 2k + 1$. Then, no column in the network receives both $\mathbf{x}_i$ and $\mathbf{x}_j$ as input. When we replace one b with an a, the value of $\mathbf{h}_+$ remains the same. Since the value of $\mathbf{h}_+$ (26) fully determines acceptance, the network does not accept this new string. However, the string now contains exactly one b, so we reach a contradiction. □

Definition E.1 (Strictly k-local grammar). A strictly k-local grammar over an alphabet Σ is a set of allowable k-grams S. Each $s \in S$ takes the form

$$s \in \left(\Sigma \cup \{\#\}\right)^k$$

where $\#$ is a padding symbol for the start and end of sentences.

Definition E.2 (Strictly local acceptance). A strictly k-local grammar S accepts a string σ if, at each index i,

$$\sigma_i\sigma_{i+1}..\sigma_{i+k-1} \in S.$$

Lemma E.2 (Implies Theorem 5.2). *A k-CNN can asymptotically accept any strictly $2k+1$-local language.*

Proof. We construct a k-CNN to simulate a strictly $2k+1$-local grammar. In the convolutional layer (25), each filter identifies whether a particular invalid $2k+1$-gram is matched. This condition is a conjunction of one-hot terms, so we use $\tanh$ to construct a linear transformation that comes out to 1 if a particular invalid sequence is matched, and -1 otherwise.

Next, the pooling layer (26) collapses the filter values at each time step. A pooled filter will be 1 if the invalid sequence it detects was matched somewhere and -1 otherwise.

Finally, we decide acceptance (27) by verifying that no invalid pattern was detected. To do this, we assign each filter a weight of -1 use a threshold of $-K + \frac{1}{2}$ where K is the number of invalid patterns. If any filter has value 1, then this sum will be negative. Otherwise, it will be $\frac{1}{2}$. Thus, asymptotic sigmoid will give us a correct acceptance decision. □

F Neural Stack Lemmas

Refer to Hao et al. (2018) for a definition of the StackNN architecture. The architecture utilizes a differentiable data structure called a *neural stack*. We show that this data structure has $2^{\Theta(n)}$ state complexity.

Lemma F.1 (Neural stack state complexity). *Let* $\mathbf{S}_n \in \mathbb{R}^{nk}$ *be a neural stack with a feedforward controller. Then,*

$$\mathcal{M}(\mathbf{S}_n) = 2^{\Theta(n)}.$$

Proof. By the general state complexity bound (Theorem A.2), we know that $\mathbb{M}(\mathbf{S}_n) = 2^{O(n)}$. We now show the lower bound.

The stack at time step n is a matrix $\mathbf{S}_n \in \mathbb{R}^{nk}$ where the rows correspond to vectors that have been pushed during the previous time steps. We set the weights of the controller θ such that, at each step, we pop with strength 0 and push $\mathbf{x}_t$ with strength 1. Then, we have

$$\mathbb{M}(\mathbf{S}_n^\theta) = |\Sigma|^n \tag{53}$$

$$\therefore \mathbb{M}(\mathbf{S}_n) = 2^{\Omega(n)}. \tag{54}$$

□

Grammatical Sequence Prediction for Real-Time Neural Semantic Parsing

Chunyang Xiao
Bloomberg
London
United Kingdom
cxiao35@bloomberg.net

Christoph Teichmann
Bloomberg
London
United Kingdom
cteichmann1@bloomberg.net

Konstantine Arkoudas
Bloomberg
New York
USA
karkoudas@bloomberg.net

Abstract

While sequence-to-sequence (seq2seq) models achieve state-of-the-art performance in many natural language processing tasks, they can be too slow for real-time applications. One performance bottleneck is predicting the most likely next token over a large vocabulary; methods to circumvent this bottleneck are a current research topic. We focus specifically on using seq2seq models for semantic parsing, where we observe that grammars often exist which specify valid formal representations of utterance semantics. By developing a generic approach for restricting the predictions of a seq2seq model to grammatically permissible continuations, we arrive at a widely applicable technique for speeding up semantic parsing. The technique leads to a 74% speed-up on an in-house dataset with a large vocabulary, compared to the same neural model without grammatical restrictions.

1 Introduction

Executable semantic parsing is the task of mapping an utterance to a logical form (LF) that can be executed against a data store (such as a SQL database or a knowledge graph), or interpreted by a computer program in some other way.[1] Various authors have tackled this task via sequence-to-sequence (seq2seq) models, which have already led to substantial advances in machine translation. These models learn to directly map the input utterance into a linearised representation of the corresponding LF, predicting it token by token. Seq2seq approaches have yielded state-of-the-art accuracy on both classic (e.g., Geoquery (Zelle and Mooney, 1996) and Atis (Dahl et al., 1994)) and more recent semantic parsing datasets (e.g., WebQuestions, WikiSQL and Spider) (Liang et al., 2017; Dong and Lapata, 2016, 2018; Yin and Neubig, 2018; Yu et al., 2018). The recent datasets are of much larger scale, which not only enables the use of more data-hungry models, such as deep neural networks, but also provides more complex challenges for semantic parsing.

The material presented in this paper was motivated by a question-answering dataset for equity search in a financial data and analytics system. We will refer to this dataset as "the EQS dataset" going forward (and we will refer to "equity search" as EQS for short). The queries in the dataset pertain to equity stocks; they are usually of the form *Show me companies that satisfy such-and-such criteria*, or *What are the top 10 companies that* $\cdots$*?*, and so on. The dataset pairs such queries with logical forms that capture their semantics. These logical forms are designed to be readily translatable into an executable query language in order to retrieve the corresponding answers from a data store in the back end. Questions can involve a large number of diverse search criteria, such as price, earnings per share, country of domicile, membership in indices, trading in specific exchanges, etc., applied to a large set of equities for which the system offers information.

The large number of search criteria and entities is reflected in the LFs, leading to a problem common with newer, more complex semantic-parsing datasets: having to deal with a large LF vocabulary size. In the EQS dataset the LF vocabulary has a size that exceeds 50,000. Since seq2seq models apply some operation over the whole vocabulary – usually the softmax operation – when deciding what symbol to output next, large LF vocabularies can slow them down considerably. For example, we observe in our EQS experiments with seq2seq models that it takes on average between 250 and 300 milliseconds to parse a query, which is too slow for one single component in a larger, real-

[1] From here on we will refer to executable semantic parsing simply as semantic parsing.

Proceedings of the Workshop on Deep Learning and Formal Languages: Building Bridges, pages 14–23
Florence, Italy, August, 2nd 2019.

time question-answering pipeline. This is consistent with observations made previously in the neural language modelling literature; see for example Bengio et al. (2003); Mikolov et al. (2010), where the authors show that when the vocabulary size exceeds a certain threshold, the softmax calculation becomes the computational bottleneck.

Our proposal for tackling this bottleneck is based on the fact that there generally exist grammars, which we call *LF grammars*, specifying the concrete syntax of valid logical forms (LFs). This is usually the case because LFs need to be machine-readable. We further note that, for a given LF prefix, one can usually use the LF grammar to look up the next grammatically permissible tokens (i.e., tokens that are part of a grammatically valid completion of the prefix). For example, if the language of valid LFs can be expressed by a context-free grammar (CFG), as is almost always the case, then look-ups could be performed with an online version of the Earley parser (Earley, 1970). If it is possible to efficiently look up the permissible next tokens for a given prefix, then restricting the softmax operation to those permissible tokens should improve efficiency, and because only non-permissible tokens are ruled out, this will only ever prevent the system from producing invalid LFs.

If the number of grammatically permissible tokens at some prediction step is substantially smaller than the LF's vocabulary size, the integration of the LF grammar may reduce prediction time for that step significantly. In semantic parsing problems a grammar can naturally lead to prediction steps with few choices. To see why this might be the case, consider our LFs in Figure 1, which involve atomic constraints of the form:

$$(\textit{field operator value}).$$

While there are many grammatically permissible choices for *field* and *value*, the choices for *operator* are rather limited.[2] LFs for many applications will contain "structural" elements with a limited number of choices in grammatically predictable positions, and we can use grammars to exploit this fact.

In order to make the computation of permissible next tokens efficient, we propose to use a finite-state automaton (FSA) approximation of the LF grammar. Finite-state automata can capture local

[2]Equality, less than and so on.

Query: return on capital sp500
LF: (AND
    (FLD_INDEX EQ enumValue(IDX_SP500))
    (display FLD_RETURN_ON_CAP))
Query: steel western europe not german
LF: (AND
    (NOT (FLD_DOMICILE EQ enumValue(COU_GERMANY)))
    (FLD_DOMICILE EQ enumValue(COU_WESTERN_EUROPE))
    (FLD_EQS_SECTOR EQ enumValue(SEC_GICS_STEEL)))

Figure 1: Two (query, LF) pairs in the EQS dataset.

relations that are often quite predictive of the admissible tokens in a given context, and can therefore lead to considerable speed improvements for our setting, even if we use an approximate grammar. Moreover, approximations can be designed in such a way that a FSA accepts a superset of the actual LF language, preserving the guarantee that only ill-formed LFs will ever be ruled out.

In this paper we therefore work with a grammar for which the next permissible tokens can be computed efficiently, and show how such a grammar can be combined with a seq2seq model in order to substantially improve the efficiency of inference. While we focus on using FSAs to restrict a recurrent neural network with attention in the EQS dataset, our approach is generic and could be used to speed up any sequential prediction model with any grammar that allows for efficient computation of next-token sets. Our experiments show that in our domain of interest we obtain a reduction in parsing time by up to 74%.

2 Logical Forms and their Grammar

2.1 Equity search

The domain of interest is that of *equity search*, or *EQS* for short, in which queries are intended to screen for companies[3] that satisfy certain criteria, such as being domiciled in a certain country or region (such as France or North America), being in a certain sector (such as the automobile or technology sectors), being members of a certain index (such as the S&P 500), being traded in certain exchanges (such as the London or Oslo stock exchanges), or their fundamental financial indicators (such as market capitalization or earnings per share) satisfying certain simple numeric criteria.

[3]Or more precisely, for tradeable equity *tickers* such as `IBM` or `FB`.

Some sample queries:

- *What are the top five Asian tech companies?*
- *Show me all auto firms traded in Nysex whose market cap last quarter was over $1 billion*
- *Top 10 European non-German tech firms sorted by p/b ratio*

Queries may also be expressed in much more telegraphic style, e.g., the second query could also be phrased as *auto nysex last quarter mcap > $1bn*. The two queries in Figure 1 are additional examples of tersely formulated queries, the first one asking to display the return-on-capital for all companies in the S&P 500 index, and the second one asking for all Western European companies in the steel sector except for German companies.

The LF language we use was designed to express the search intent of a query in a clear and non-ambiguous way. In the following section we describe the abstract grammar and concrete syntax of a subset of this LF (we cannot treat every construct due to space limitations).

2.2 LF Abstract Grammar and Concrete Syntax

As with many formal logical languages, the abstract grammar of our LF naturally falls into two classes: *atomic* LFs corresponding to individual logical or operational constraints; and *complex* LFs that contain other LFs as proper parts. The former constitute the basis case of the inductive definition of the LF grammar, while the latter correspond to the recursive clauses.

Relational Atomic Constraints The main atomic constraints of interest in this domain are relational, of the form

$$(\textit{field}(t) \;\; \textit{op} \;\; \textit{value})$$

where typically *field* is either a numeric field (such as *price*); or a so-called "enum field," that is, an enumerated type. An example here would be a field such as a credit rating (say, long-term Fitch ratings), which has a a finite number of values (such as *B+*, *AAA*, etc.); or country of domicile, which also has a a finite number of values (*algeria*, *belgium*, and so on); or an index field, whose values are the major stock indices (such as the S&P 500). The *value* is a numeric value if the corresponding *field* is numeric, though it may be a *complex numeric value*, e.g., one that has currencies or denominations attached to it (such as "5 billion dollars"). The operator *op* is either equality (*EQ*), inequality (*NEQ*), less-than (*LS*), greater-than (*GR*), less-than-or-equal (*LE*), etc.[4] Note that all fields, both numeric and enum, are indexed by a time expression t, representing the value of that field at that particular time. For example, the atomic constraint

$$(\textit{price}(\textit{June}\;\; 23, 2018) = \$100)$$

states that the (closing) price on June 23, 2018 was 100 USD. We drop the time t when it is either immaterial or the respective field is not time sensitive. We omit the specification of the grammar and semantics of time expressions, since we will not be using times in what follows in order to simplify the discussion.

Display Atomic Constraints Some of our atomic constraints are operational in the sense that they represent directives about what fields to *display* as the query result, possibly along with auxiliary presentation information such as sorting order. For instance, for the query *Show me the market caps and revenues of asian tech firms*, two of the resulting constraints would be the display directives (*display FLD_MKT_CAP*) and (*display FLD_SALES_REV_TURN*).

Complex Constraints Complex constraints are boolean combinations of other constraints, obtained by applying one of the operations *NOT, OR, AND*, resulting in recursively built constraints of the form $(\textit{NOT} \;\; c)$, $(\textit{AND} \;\; c_1 \;\; c_2 \;\; \cdots \;\; c_n)$, and $(\textit{OR} \;\; c_1 \;\; c_2)$.[5]

3 Encoding LF grammar in FSAs

For efficient incremental parsing and computation of the next permissible tokens, we encode our grammar using finite state automata (FSAs). As FSAs can only produce regular languages that are strictly less expressive than context free languages such as the one recognized by our LF grammar, our strategy is to use automata to build a superset for our LF language. Some of the automata

[4] If the field is an enum, then comparison operators such as *GR* or *LE* make sense only if the field is ordered. Credit ratings are naturally ordered, but countries, for example, are not. Nevertheless, the *syntax* of constraints allows for $(\textit{france} \;\; GE \;\; 2)$; such a constraint is weeded out by *type judgments*, not by the LF grammar.

[5] We model the OR operation as binary operation and the AND operation as n-ary to make them close to the natural language syntax we observe in the dataset.

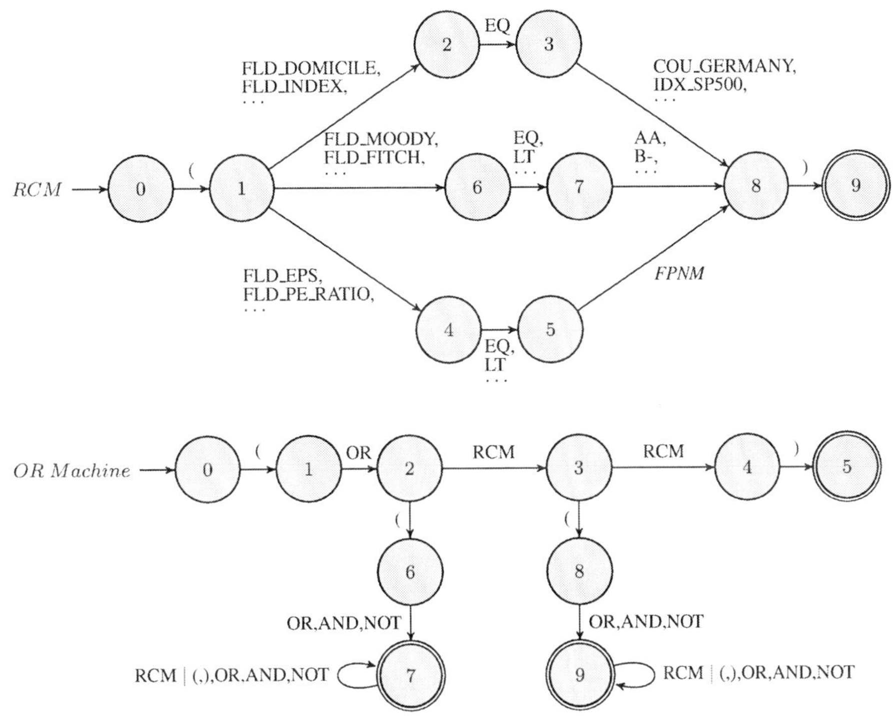

Figure 2: Some automata involved in building the supersert of the LF grammar.

involved in building this superset are shown in Figure 2. Note that, while we defined our FSA approximation manually, there exist general techniques to construct an automaton whose language is a superset of a CFG's language for any given CFG (Nederhof, 2000). This means that the approach could easily be used for any LF language that can be described by a CFG.

For all automata, we take the start states to be 0 and indicate the final states with double circles. The "|" stands for the union operation over automata. On each arc, we either specify as labels LF tokens that the FSA can consume in order to transition to its next state(s); or else we specify a previously defined machine (automaton) noted with "*M:machine_name*"[6] where the source state of the arc coincides with the start state of the automaton and its target state coincides with the final state(s) of the automaton.[7]

Relational Atomic Constraint machines The automaton *RCM* ("Relational Constraint Machine") in the top part of Figure 2 generates relational atomic constraints of the form (*field op value*); the *FPNM* (floating point number machine) is an automaton recognizing restricted floating point numbers. Note that some extra-syntactic information about fields is explicitly built into the machine. For example, if a constraint begins with an unordered enum field that only admits equality, such as *FLD_DOMICILE*, then the operator (on the arc from state 2 to state 3) is always *EQ*, whereas if the field is ordered (as all numeric fields are, and some enum fields such as ratings), then any operator may follow (such as *LE*, *GR*, etc.). The automaton constrains what follows a num field in a similar fashion.

Complex Constraint machines Unlike their atomic counterparts, logically complex constraints can be arbitrarily nested, thereby forming a nonregular context-free language that cannot be characterized by FSAs. We get around this limitation by constructing FSAs for such complex constraints that accept a regular language forming a *superset* of the proper context-free LF language. The automaton "OR Machine" in Figure 2 illustrates such a construction. This machine recognizes LFs of the form (*OR RCM RCM*) along the topmost horizontal path of the automaton (state sequence 0-1-2-3-4-5). But if one or two of these relational constraints are replaced by logically com-

[6]In that case the "arc" is just a concise representation of the entire automaton that goes by *machine_name*.

[7]In the case of multiple final states, one simply replicates the target state to coincide with each of the final states.

plex constraints, the automaton can recognize the result by taking one or two of the vertical paths (state sequences 2-6-7 and 3-8-9, respectively). These paths can also accept strings that are not syntactically valid LFs. However, we are only using these automata to restrict the softmax application to a subset of the LF vocabulary, and for that purpose these automata are conservative approximations. An alternative approach would be to use FSAs for logically complex constraints that essentially unroll nested applications of logical operators up to some fixed depth k, e.g., say $k = 2$ or 3, as logically complex constraints with more than 3 nested logical operations are exceedingly uncommon, though possible in principle. But the present approach is simple and already leads to considerable reductions in the number of permissible tokens at each prediction step, thereby significantly accelerating our neural semantic parser.

The final automaton representing the entire LF language, which we write as M_{LF}, is the union of atomic machines such as *RCM* with three "approximation" machines for the three logical operators (negation, conjunction and disjunction).

4 Combining Grammar and Neural Model

4.1 Grammatical continuations by Automata

We now show how to use the automaton M_{LF} that represents the LF grammar in order to (a) compute the set of valid next tokens, and (b) update the current prefix by appending an RNN-predicted token. We present very simple algorithms for both operations, *nextTokens* and *passToken*, which can be used with any grammar that is represented as a DFA.[8]

nextTokens: This function returns a list of the permissible next tokens based on the current automaton state, which corresponds to the current LF prefix (note that because the grammar is a DFA, there is a unique resulting state for any prefix accepted by the automaton). The function simply enumerates all the outgoing arcs from the current state and returns the corresponding labels in a list. This function is called before the token prediction model (RNN + softmax), so that its result can be used to restrict the application of softmax; the actual integration model is discussed in detail in subsection 4.2.

passToken: For any model that predicts the output in an incremental and sequential manner (e.g., RNN), we want to compute the DFA state corresponding to a partial output in a similar and lock-step fashion, so that computations in previous steps do not need to be repeated. We achieve this by maintaining a global state, called *current_state*, which is the state reached after reading the prefix that has been produced by the neural model up to this point. To update the global state, the function *passToken* is called, which simply searches for the arc ('the' again due to the DFA property) that has the currently predicted token as a label, and then transitions to the next state via that arc. Once this is done, the new global state will represent all the predictions made so far.

Time Efficiency Concerns The functions *nextTokens* and *passToken* need to be called on every step of the output's generation, and therefore need to be efficient, so that the reduction of prediction space for the token-prediction model (e.g., RNN + softmax) can lead to runtime gains. In our case, *nextTokens* returns the labels of all outgoing arcs and *passToken* performs a simple label search in addition to carrying out a state transition. All of these operations can be performed with O(1) time complexity.

4.2 Integrating Grammar into Neural Models

After calculating the permissible next tokens, we can restrict predictions in order to improve both prediction time and accuracy. We apply this general strategy to the prediction layer of our RNN-based neural network (a linear layer + softmax operation, which can be seen as a log-linear model (Dymetman and Xiao, 2016)), although it should be applicable to other prediction models, such as multi-class SVMs (Duan and Keerthi, 2005) or random forests (Ho, 1995).

Figure 3 illustrates a concrete example of integrating the grammar (represented as an automaton in our case) into the token prediction model at a particular prediction step. We focus on the prediction layer of the model, which consists of one linear layer followed by the softmax operation. The linear layer involves a matrix of size $|V| \times d$, where V is the LF vocabulary and d is the dimension of

[8] For convenience, of course, the grammar could be represented by non-deterministic automata (NFAs). The algorithms we present here would still be applicable via a simple preprocessing step that would convert the NFAs to DFAs using standard algorithms for that purpose (Rabin and Scott, 1959).

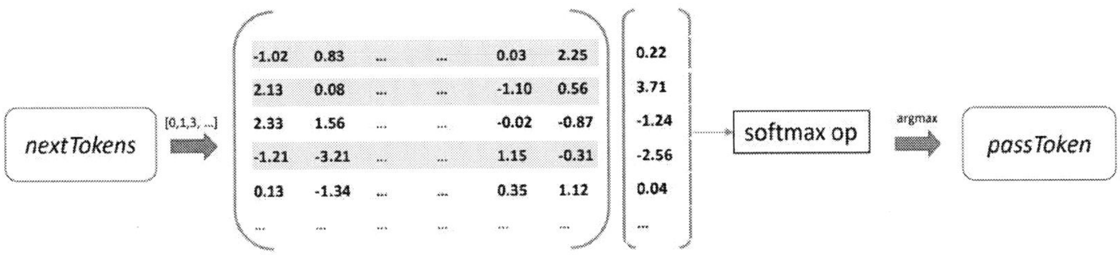

Figure 3: Integrating grammatical continuations into a log-linear model at one prediction step; rows selected by *nextTokens* are shadowed in blue.

the vector passed from the previous layer; the linear layer predicts scores for each of the V tokens before they are passed to softmax operation.

To integrate the grammar, first, the function *nextTokens* is called to return a list of tokens allowed by the grammar at this prediction step; the valid tokens are then translated into a list of indices, denoted by l_c, which is passed to the log-linear model. Supposing there are k indices in the list l_c, we can dynamically construct another matrix of size $k \times d$ where the ith row in the new matrix corresponds to the jth row in the original matrix, for $j = l_c[i]$. Figure 3 illustrates this process of choosing rows from the original matrix to construct the new matrix.

Then the new matrix-vector product will result in scores only for those k LF tokens that are permissible, and will then be passed to the softmax operation. The decision function (e.g., argmax in Figure 3) will then be applied based on the softmax score, whose results will finally be passed to *passToken* function to update the current DFA state.

Time Efficiency Concerns

We implement *nextTokens* to directly return a list of indices to avoid the cost of converting tokens to indices. We implemented our token prediction model in PyTorch, which supports slicing operations so that our on-the-fly matrix construction does not need to copy the original matrix data, but can instead just point to it. However, we find in our experiments that even matrix construction using slicing tends to be costly (see section 5).

To overcome this, we observe that we can enumerate the lists returned by *nextTokens* for every DFA state, and then cache the corresponding matrices. For example, consider RCM (the Relational Constraint Machine) in 2. We can cache the value of *nextTokens* for state 1 by precomputing the matrix corresponding to all the enum/num fields. Doing this caching for every DFA state can be expensive in memory; in practice, one may consider tradeoffs between memory consumption and prediction time.

5 Model and Experiments

5.1 EQS Dataset

Our experiments are conducted on the EQS dataset. The dataset consists of queries paired with their LFs, which were obtained in a semi-automated manner. The dataset contains 1981 (NL, LF) pairs as training data and 331 (NL, LF) pairs as test data. The LF vocabulary size is 56209, most of which consists of enum field names and values. All the LFs can be accepted by the FSA discussed in Section 3.

The dataset is too small to effectively learn a model that can reliably predict rare fields or values. However, as most of the queries involve only common fields and entities, we find in our experiments that our neural semantic parser is able to parse a large number of those queries correctly; orthogonal research is being conducted on how to handle more rare fields or entities.

5.2 Baseline Neural Model

We use a seq2seq neural architecture as our baseline. For our encoder, we initialize the word embeddings using Glove vectors (Pennington et al., 2014); then a Bi-LSTM is run over the question where the last output is used to represent the meaning of the question. For the decoder, we again use an LSTM that runs over LF prefixes, where the LF token embeddings are learned during training. Our decoder is equipped with an attention mechanism (Luong et al., 2015) used to attend over the output of the Bi-LSTM encoder. We use greedy decoding to predict the LFs.

We choose hyperparameters based on our previous experience with this dataset. The word and LF token embeddings have 150 dimensions. The Bi-LSTM encoder is of dimension 150 for its hidden vector in each direction, therefore the decoding LSTM is of dimension 300 for its hidden vector. We train the model with RMSprop (Tieleman and Hinton, 2012) for 50 epochs.

Our baseline neural model achieves 80.33% accuracy on the test set. Most of the errors made by our model are due to unseen fields or values; we observe that our model also fails on queries involving compositionality patterns that have not been seen in training, a problem similar to those reported by (Lake and Baroni, 2018).

5.3 Experimental Setups

All our experiments were conducted on a server with 40 Intel Xeon@3.00GHz CPUs and 380 GB of RAM. We monitor the server state closely while conducting the experiments.

Our models are implemented in PyTorch (Paszke et al., 2017), which is able to exploit the server's multi-core architecture. The peak usage for both CPU load and memory consumption for all our models is far below the server's capacity.

We run all the models over the entire test dataset (331 sentences) and report the average prediction time for each sentence. For each model, we conduct 5 such runs to calculate the standard deviations of different runs. The standard deviations are small in absolute and relative value.

5.4 Results

Integrating the LF grammar into prediction at decoding time eliminates all grammatical errors and can therefore improve accuracy. This has been shown, for example, by Xiao et al. (2016); Yin and Neubig (2018), and indeed we obtain similar accuracy improvements. By incorporating the grammar at decoding time at all decoding steps (using its superset represented as an automaton), our parser is able to eliminate some grammatical errors, achieving 80.67% accuracy on the test set, which improves our baseline model by 0.30%.

Table 1 shows the main results of our experiments. Our baseline neural semantic parser (NSP) takes on average 0.260 seconds to predict the LF for a given query. When we use the model that

Model	Avg. time	Avg. tokens
NSP	0.260 ± 0.002	56209
NSP-G(500)	0.079 ± 0.000	9643
NSP-G(10^4)	0.252 ± 0.000	6981
NSP-G(all)	4.416 ± 0.029	**6336**
NSP-GC(500)	0.074 ± 0.000	9643
NSP-GC(10^4)	0.069 ± 0.000	6981
NSP-GC(all)	$\mathbf{0.067 \pm 0.000}$	**6336**

Table 1: Prediction time (in seconds) and number of permissible tokens per query on average, for our baseline neural semantic parser (NSP) and various models using grammar integration with caching (NSP-GC) or without (NSP-G).

integrates the LF grammar but constructs the reduced matrices on the fly (GSP-G), we find that despite the reduction of average permissible tokens (from 56209 to 6336), the prediction time actually increases drastically to 4.416 seconds.

To shed some light on this, we integrate the grammatically permissible next tokens only when their number is (a) less than 500 and (b) less than 10^4. We observe that when the number of permissible next tokens is small, as in case (a), integrating the grammar can indeed reduce prediction time, indicating that the slowing is due to the dynamic matrix construction that uses the PyTorch slicing operation, as *nextTokens* and *passToken* are called at every prediction step in all cases.

To avoid this, we cache the reduced matrices (subsection 4.2, NSP-GC in Table 1) and observe that prediction time decreases in this case when more grammar integration is applied. The best prediction time (0.067 second per query) is achieved by NSP-GC when the grammar is used at every step. But similar speed-ups can be achieved when we are using cached matrices only for states with a small *nextTokens* set.

6 Related Work

Speeding up neural models that have a softmax bottleneck is an ongoing research problem in NLP. In machine translation, some approaches tackle the problem by moving from the prediction of word-level units to sub-word units (Sennrich et al., 2016) or characters (Chung et al., 2016). This approach can reduce the dimensionality of the softmax significantly, at the price of increasing the number of output steps and thus requiring the model to learn more long-distance dependencies between its outputs. The technique could easily be combined with the one described here; the only adaptation required would be to change the grammar so that it uses smaller units to define its language. In a finite-state context, this would mean replacing transitions corresponding to a single LF token with a sequence of transitions that construct the token from characters. This creates potential for memory savings as well, if states in these expanded transitions can be shared in a trie structure.

Another approach for ameliorating a softmax bottleneck is the use of a hierarchical softmax (Morin and Bengio, 2005), which is based on organizing all possible output values into a hierarchy or tree of clusters. A token to be emitted is chosen by starting at the root cluster and then picking a child cluster until a leaf is reached. A token in this leaf cluster is then selected. Our approach could be combined with the hierarchical softmax method by creating a specific version of the cluster hierarchy to be associated with every state. We would filter all impossible tokens for a state from the leaf clusters and then prune away empty clusters in a bottom-up fashion to obtain a specific cluster.

While they have not been used in order to speed up predictions, grammars describing possible output structures have been combined with neural models in a number of recent papers on semantic parsing (Yin and Neubig, 2017, 2018; Krishnamurthy et al., 2017; Xiao et al., 2016, 2017). These papers use grammars to guide the training of the neural network model and to restrict the decisions the model can make at training and prediction time in order to obtain more accurate results with less data. Our approach is focused on speed improvements and does not require any changes to the underlying model or training protocols.

Like our approach, the one presented by L'Hostis et al. (2016) for machine translation tries to limit the decoding vocabulary. Their approach relies on limiting the tokens allowed during decoding to those that co-occurred frequently with the tokens in the input. Because this might rule out tokens that are needed to construct the correct output, this may decrease model performance. Our approach is guaranteed to never rule out correct outputs. For additional performance gains it should be possible to combine both approaches.

7 Future Work

We have used superset approximations based on finite-state automata instead of directly using the grammar of the LF language, which will usually be context-free. This choice is driven by the need for an efficient implementation of *passToken* and *nextTokens*, which could be expensive for longer sequences when using a general context-free grammar. However, for those context-free grammars that are LR (Knuth, 1965), recognition can be performed in linear time, and it is easy to see that both *passToken* and *nextTokens* can then be implemented with O(1) time complexity on average. Furthermore, the caching mechanism we have proposed for *nextTokens* in this work is applicable in the case of LR grammars. Therefore, it would be possible to implement the methods proposed here for any LR grammar, and such grammars cover most LF languages in practical use.[9]

For most LF languages there will be restrictions on the logical types of expressions that can occur in certain positions. We can detect some of these restrictions in our finite-state automata, but in general a type system could capture well-formedness conditions that cannot be easily expressed with FSAs, or even in context-free grammars. It would be interesting to investigate how more expressive type checking can be integrated into our present framework in a more general setting.

8 Conclusion

We propose a method to improve the time efficiency of seq2seq models for semantic parsing using a large vocabulary. We show that one can leverage a finite-state approximation to the LF language in order to speed up neural parsing significantly. Given a context-free grammar for the LF language, our strategy is general and can be applied to any model that predicts the output in a sequential manner.

In the future we will explore alternatives to finite-state automata, which potentially characterize the relevant LF languages exactly while still allowing for efficient computation of admissible next tokens. We also plan to experiment with additional datasets.

Acknowledgments

We would like to thank Mohamed Yahya for a number of insightful comments and suggestions.

[9]The reason being that most LF languages are designed to be machine-readable and akin to programming languages, so they tend to be unambiguous (e.g., they are fully parenthesized) and readily parsable.

References

Yoshua Bengio, Réjean Ducharme, Pascal Vincent, and Christian Janvin. 2003. A neural probabilistic language model. *Journal of Machine Learning Research*, 3:1137–1155.

Junyoung Chung, Kyunghyun Cho, and Yoshua Bengio. 2016. A character-level decoder without explicit segmentation for neural machine translation. In *Proceedings of the 54th Annual Meeting of the Association for Computational Linguistics*, pages 1693–1703.

Deborah A. Dahl, Madeleine Bates, Michael Brown, William Fisher, Kate Hunicke-Smith, David Pallett, Christine Pao, Alexander Rudnicky, and Elizabeth Shriberg. 1994. Expanding the scope of the atis task: The atis-3 corpus. In *Proceedings of the Workshop on Human Language Technology*, pages 43–48.

Li Dong and Mirella Lapata. 2016. Language to logical form with neural attention. In *Proceedings of the 54th Annual Meeting of the Association for Computational Linguistics*, pages 33–43.

Li Dong and Mirella Lapata. 2018. Coarse-to-fine decoding for neural semantic parsing. In *Proceedings of the 56th Annual Meeting of the Association for Computational Linguistics*, pages 731–742.

Kai-Bo Duan and S. Sathiya Keerthi. 2005. Which is the best multiclass svm method? an empirical study. In *Proceedings of the 6th International Conference on Multiple Classifier Systems*, pages 278–285.

Marc Dymetman and Chunyang Xiao. 2016. Log-linear rnns: Towards recurrent neural networks with flexible prior knowledge. *CoRR*, abs/1607.02467.

Jay Earley. 1970. An efficient context-free parsing algorithm. *Communications of the ACM*, 13(2):94–102.

Tin Kam Ho. 1995. Random decision forests. In *Proceedings of the Third International Conference on Document Analysis and Recognition*, pages 278–282.

Donald E. Knuth. 1965. On the translation of languages from left to right. *Information and Control*, 8(6):607–639.

Jayant Krishnamurthy, Pradeep Dasigi, and Matt Gardner. 2017. Neural semantic parsing with type constraints for semi-structured tables. In *Proceedings of the 2017 Conference on Empirical Methods in Natural Language Processing*, pages 1516–1526.

Brenden M. Lake and Marco Baroni. 2018. Generalization without systematicity: On the compositional skills of sequence-to-sequence recurrent networks. In *Proceedings of the 35th International Conference on Machine Learning*, pages 2879–2888.

Gurvan L'Hostis, David Grangier, and Michael Auli. 2016. Vocabulary selection strategies for neural machine translation. *CoRR*, abs/1610.00072.

Chen Liang, Jonathan Berant, Quoc Le, Kenneth D. Forbus, and Ni Lao. 2017. Neural symbolic machines: Learning semantic parsers on freebase with weak supervision. In *Proceedings of the 55th Annual Meeting of the Association for Computational Linguistics*, pages 23–33.

Thang Luong, Hieu Pham, and Christopher D. Manning. 2015. Effective approaches to attention-based neural machine translation. In *Proceedings of the 2015 Conference on Empirical Methods in Natural Language Processing*, pages 1412–1421.

Tomas Mikolov, Martin Karafiát, Lukás Burget, Jan Cernocký, and Sanjeev Khudanpur. 2010. Recurrent neural network based language model. In *Interspeech*, pages 1045–1048.

Frederic Morin and Yoshua Bengio. 2005. Hierarchical probabilistic neural network language model. In *Proceedings of the Tenth International Workshop on Artificial Intelligence and Statistics*, pages 246–252.

Mark-Jan Nederhof. 2000. Practical experiments with regular approximation of context-free languages. *Computational Linguistics*, 26(1):17–44.

Adam Paszke, Sam Gross, Soumith Chintala, Gregory Chanan, Edward Yang, Zachary DeVito, Zeming Lin, Alban Desmaison, Luca Antiga, and Adam Lerer. 2017. Automatic differentiation in pytorch. In *NIPS 2017 Workshop Autodiff*.

Jeffrey Pennington, Richard Socher, and Christopher Manning. 2014. Glove: Global vectors for word representation. In *Proceedings of the 2014 Conference on Empirical Methods in Natural Language Processing*, pages 1532–1543.

M. O. Rabin and D. Scott. 1959. Finite automata and their decision problems. *IBM Journal of Research and Development*, 3(2):114–125.

Rico Sennrich, Barry Haddow, and Alexandra Birch. 2016. Neural machine translation of rare words with subword units. In *Proceedings of the 54th Annual Meeting of the Association for Computational Linguistics*, pages 1715–1725.

T. Tieleman and G. Hinton. 2012. Lecture 6.5—RmsProp: Divide the gradient by a running average of its recent magnitude. COURSERA: Neural Networks for Machine Learning.

Chunyang Xiao, Marc Dymetman, and Claire Gardent. 2016. Sequence-based structured prediction for semantic parsing. In *Proceedings of the 54th Annual Meeting of the Association for Computational Linguistics*, pages 1341–1350.

Chunyang Xiao, Marc Dymetman, and Claire Gardent. 2017. Symbolic priors for rnn-based semantic parsing. In *Proceedings of the Twenty-Sixth International Joint Conference on Artificial Intelligence, IJCAI-17*, pages 4186–4192.

Pengcheng Yin and Graham Neubig. 2017. A syntactic neural model for general-purpose code generation. In *Proceedings of the 55th Annual Meeting of the Association for Computational Linguistics*, pages 440–450.

Pengcheng Yin and Graham Neubig. 2018. Tranx: A transition-based neural abstract syntax parser for semantic parsing and code generation. In *Proceedings of the 2018 Conference on Empirical Methods in Natural Language Processing: System Demonstrations*, pages 7–12.

Tao Yu, Michihiro Yasunaga, Kai Yang, Rui Zhang, Dongxu Wang, Zifan Li, and Dragomir R. Radev. 2018. Syntaxsqlnet: Syntax tree networks for complex and cross-domaintext-to-sql task. In *Proceedings of the 2018 Conference on Empirical Methods in Natural Language Processing*, pages 1653–1663.

John M. Zelle and Raymond J. Mooney. 1996. Learning to parse database queries using inductive logic programming. In *Proceedings of the Thirteenth National Conference on Artificial Intelligence*, AAAI 96, pages 1050–1055.

Relating RNN layers with the spectral WFA ranks in sequence modelling

Farhana Ferdousi Liza
School of Computing
University of Kent
Canterbury, CT2 7NF, UK
fl207@kent.ac.uk

Marek Grzes
School of Computing
University of Kent
Canterbury, CT2 7NF, UK
m.grzes@kent.ac.uk

Abstract

We analyse Recurrent Neural Networks (RNNs) to understand the significance of multiple LSTM layers. We argue that the Weighted Finite-state Automata (WFA) trained using a spectral learning algorithm are helpful to analyse RNNs. Our results suggest that multiple LSTM layers in RNNs help learning distributed hidden states, but have a smaller impact on the ability to learn long-term dependencies. The analysis is based on the empirical results, however relevant theory (whenever possible) was discussed to justify and support our conclusions.

1 Introduction

Sequence prediction is a problem that involves using historical sequence data (i.e. context) to predict the next symbol or symbols in the sequence. Weighted Finite-state Automata (WFA) and Recurrent Neural Networks (RNNs) provide a general framework for the representation of functions that map strings (i.e. sequential data) to real numbers. Nondeterministic Weighted Finite-state Automata (WFA) map input words to real numbers and are not guaranteed to be tractable (Avni and Kupferman, 2015; Sharan et al., 2017). In general, WFA use hidden states and learning is usually done by the Expectation-Maximisation (EM) algorithm, which is computationally expensive and does not come with a guarantee of global optimality. Spectral learning algorithms for WFA (Balle et al., 2014) provide an alternative to EM that is both computationally efficient and statistically consistent. On the other hand, RNNs are remarkably expressive models. Even a single-layer RNN network has powerful sequence modelling capacity. RNNs are also Turing complete and can represent any computable function (Siegelmann and Sontag, 1991), but the theoretical analysis of even a single-layer RNN is difficult.

Existing research shows that multilayer RNNs are advantageous for efficient sequence modelling (Zaremba et al., 2014; Jozefowicz et al., 2015). However, it is hard to analyse such models theoretically. As a result, in spite of competitive empirical results, it is not clear what kind of additional modelling power is gained by a deep architecture (i.e. more than one hidden layer in RNNs). Stacking RNN layers (in space) is inspired by the multilayer perceptron (MLP) and the hypothesis Bengio et al. (2009) that multiple layers allow the model to have greater complexity by incorporating complex feature representations of each time step. This allows each recurrent level to operate at a different time-scale. For the non-recurrent networks, Bengio et al. (2009) hypothesise that a deep, hierarchical model can be exponentially more efficient at representing some functions than a shallow one. Theoretical (Le Roux and Bengio, 2010; Delalleau and Bengio, 2011; Pascanu et al., 2013) and empirical (Goodfellow et al., 2013; Hinton et al., 2012) work on non-recurrent networks agrees with the above hypothesis. Based on these results, Pascanu et al. (2014) assumed that the MLP-based hypothesis proposed by Bengio et al. (2009) is also true for the recurrent neural networks. The earlier work attempted at capturing large context and reducing the training time by using multilayer RNNs. For example, El Hihi and Bengio (1996) assumed that the layers increase the capacity of learning the context by capturing the improved long-term history, whereas Schmidhuber (2008) argues that the stacked RNN requires less computation per time-step and far fewer training sequences than a single-layer RNN.

Elman (1990) introduced the notion of 'memory' to capture non-fixed long-term contexts through the recurrent layer. When stacking the RNNs, the transition between the consecutive recurrent layers is still shallow (Pascanu et al.,

Proceedings of the Workshop on Deep Learning and Formal Languages: Building Bridges, pages 24–33
Florence, Italy, August, 2nd 2019. ©2019 Association for Computational Linguistics

2014). Thus, stacking the RNNs does not extend the hypothesis of (Bengio et al., 2009) to the recurrent layer that is dedicated for long-term context capture. The empirical results of Zaremba et al. (2014); Jozefowicz et al. (2015) suggested that multilayer RNNs improve sequence modelling. We show empirical evidence that indicates that a multilayer RNN does capture better context as shown by El Hihi and Bengio (1996), but that is achieved across stacked layers instead of the time scale (i.e. instead of recurrent layer). Better learning depends on capturing the improved input representation at each time step and capturing improved long-term dependency from the previous time-steps in a sequence. In this paper, we investigate RNN learning from the formal language perspective using the WFA models, and we show that adding more layers may not be sufficient if the model has to deal with long-term dependencies.

WFA-based models are used for both theoretical studies and sequence prediction tasks including language modelling (Buchsbaum et al., 1998). Evaluating their performance on real and synthetic data can help us to understand the model's hidden state relationship with the RNN layers. In the existing literature, stacking multiple RNN layers (in space) is used to obtain improved accuracy on sequence prediction tasks, but this is done without deeply-justified reasons of such choices. Our experiments and analysis show that the hidden states of a process can be modelled efficiently using multiple layers, but multiple layers may not be sufficient to model long-term dependencies in sequential observations.

In this paper, we use two types of RNN models (one is a single-layer and another is a two-layer stacked RNN network) and a WFA. All methods were evaluated on fifteen datasets to answer the following question "what is the impact of multiple RNN layers in sequence modelling?". To answer this question, we contrasted the impact of the LSTM layers in RNNs with the rank (i.e. the number of hidden states) in the corresponding WFA models.

2 Data

In this section we introduce the 15 datasets used in the Sequence PredIction ChallengE (SPiCe) in 2016. The datasets consist of 8 synthetic (fully or partially) and 7 real-world datasets. Among the synthetic datasets, four are generated artificially and four are partially synthetic based on real data. Datasets are publicly available[1] and descriptions can be found in (Balle et al., 2017). Our numbering of datasets is consistent with SPiCe'16. The synthetic datasets 1, 2, and 3 were artificially generated based on a Hidden Markov Model (HMM) (Balle et al., 2017). HMM sequences were generated with n states and non-stationary transition probabilities were obtained by partitioning the unit interval [0,1) into n equal sub-intervals and letting the states evolve as $h_{t+1} = h_t + \Phi \bmod 1$, for some irrational number Φ. The emission probabilities were sampled from a Dirichlet distribution. Another synthetic dataset, 12, consists of synthetic data generated using the PAutomaC data generator (Verwer et al., 2014b). Partially synthetic datasets 6 and 9 are based on software engineering and come from the challenge RERS 2013 (Howar et al., 2014). Partially synthetic datasets 14 and 15 contain synthetic data generated from two Deterministic Finite State Automata learned using the ALERGIA algorithm (Carrasco and Oncina, 1994) based on the NLP datasets 4 and 5, respectively.

Real datasets 4 (English Verbs from Penn Treebank), 5 (Character Language Modelling benchmark from Penn Treebank), and 8 (POS from Ancora) all correspond to NLP problems from Penn Treebank (Marcus et al., 1993a) and the Spanish Ancora corpus (Taulé et al., 2008). Dataset 11 (lemmalisation) was created from a lemmatised version of the Fickr-8k dataset (Hodosh et al., 2013). Real dataset 13 (spelling correction) was derived from a Twitter spelling correction corpus (twi, 2010). Real datasets 7 and 10 are protein families sequences taken from the Pfam database (Finn et al., 2015).

3 Sequence Modelling and Evaluation

The Sequence Predictlction ChallengE (SPiCe) (Balle et al., 2017) was an on-line competition to predict the next element of a sequence. The competition scored methods on their performance on both real and synthetic data (see Sec. 2). Training datasets consist of whole sequences and the aim is to learn a model that allows the ranking of potential next symbols for a given test sequence (prefix or context), that is, the most likely options for a single next symbol. Once rankings for all prefixes were submitted by the participants, the score

[1] http://spice.lif.univ-mrs.fr/data.php

($NDCG_5$ explained below) of the submission was computed. The score is a ranking metric based on normalised discounted cumulative gain computed from the ranking of 5 potential next symbols starting from the most probable one. Suppose the test set is made of prefixes $y_1, \ldots, y_M$ and the distinct next symbols ranking submitted for y_i is $(\hat{a}_1^i, \ldots, \hat{a}_5^i)$ sorted from more likely to least likely. The target probability distribution of possible next symbols given the prefix y_i, $p(.|y_i)$, was known to the organisers. Thus, the exact measure for prefix y_i could be computed using the following equation:

$$NDCG_5(\hat{a}_1^i, \ldots, \hat{a}_5^i) = \frac{\sum_{k=1}^{5} \frac{p(\hat{a}_k^i|y_i)}{log_2(k+1)}}{\sum_{k=1}^{5} \frac{p_k}{log_2(k+1)}}$$

where $p_1 \geq p_2 \geq \ldots \geq p_5$ are the top 5 values in the distribution $p(.|y_i)$. More details on this evaluation can be found in (Balle et al., 2017).

4 WFA Models

WFA represent functions for mapping strings to real numbers. WFA include as special instances Deterministic Finite-state Automata (DFAs), hidden Markov models (HMMs), and predictive state representations (PSRs).

Let Σ^* denote the set of strings over a finite alphabet Σ and let λ be the empty word. A WFA with k states is a tuple $A = \langle a_0, a_\infty, A_\sigma \rangle$ where $a_0, a_\infty \in \mathbf{R}^k$ are the initial and final weight vectors respectively, and $A_\sigma \in \mathbf{k} \times \mathbf{k}$ is the transition matrix for each symbol $\sigma \in \Sigma$. A WFA computes a function $f_A : \Sigma^* \to \mathbf{R}$ defined for each word $x = x_1 x_2 \ldots x_n \in \Sigma^*$ by $f_{A(x)} = {a_o}^\top A_{x_1} A_{x_2} \ldots A_{x_n} a_\infty$.

A WFA A with k states is minimal if its number of states is minimal, i.e., any WFA B such that $f_A = f_B$ has at least k states. A function $f : \Sigma^* \to R$ is recognisable if it can be computed by a WFA. In this case the rank of f is the number of states of a minimal WFA computing f. Note that this is the key reason why rank (i.e. the number of hidden states) is an important parameter that we exploit in this paper. If f is not recognisable, we let rank(f) = ∞.

Approximating distributions over strings is a hard learning problem. Learning WFA has exponential computational complexity (Mohri, 2004). The recent advancement in learning WFA is based on spectral learning, which reduces the computation complexity of learning WFA (Balle et al., 2014).

In this paper we use a Hankel matrix based spectral learning algorithm for WFA. The basic steps of the algorithm are as follows:

S1. Basis Selection: Choose a set of prefixes P and suffixes S

S2. Build a Hankel matrix: The Hankel matrix ($H_f \in \mathbf{R}^{\Sigma^* \times \Sigma^*}$) associated with a function $f : \Sigma^* \to \mathbf{R}$ is a bi-infinite matrix . In practice, one deals with finite sub-blocks of the Hankel matrix based on the chosen basis in S1, thus $B = (P, S) \subset \Sigma^* \times \Sigma^*$. The corresponding sub-block of the Hankel matrix is denoted by $H \in R^{|P| \times |S|}$. The entry $H(p, s)$ is the value of the target function on the sequence obtained by concatenating prefix p with suffix s. Among all possible basis, we are particularly interested in the ones with the same rank as f. We say that a basis is complete if $rank(H) = rank(f) = rank(H_f)$.

S3. Perform SVD on $H = u \sigma v^\top$.

S4. Use the factorization $F = u\sigma$, $B = v^\top$ and H to recover the parameters of the minimal WFA, following (Hsu et al., 2012, see Sec. 2.3).

The hyperparameters of the learning algorithm (Balle et al., 2014) for retrieving the parameters of the minimum WFA are the number of states n of the target WFA and the basis (i.e. sets of P and S). This n is also a rank of the n-dimensional reconstruction of the Hankel matrix when the best n dimensions of its SVD are used.

We choose a basis that contains most frequent elements (substrings) observed in the sample based on the work by Balle et al. (2012) as this approach was found computationally efficient. The rows and columns of the Hankel matrix correspond to the substrings, and the cells of the Hankel matrix contain the frequencies of the corresponding substrings. In this approach, the length of these substrings along rows (nR) and along column (nC) are also the hyperparameters of the spectral learning algorithm for WFA (Balle et al., 2014).

4.1 Tuning Hyperparameters

Similar to Larochelle et al. (2007), our tuning method included a combination of multiresolution search, coordinate ascent, and manual search, with a significant utilisation of the last method. On all datasets, our method first initialises nR and nC to 4 and n to 5. Note that the actual number of rows (columns) in the Hankel matrix is much larger than nR (nC). In the second step, the algorithm starts the process of tuning the number of states n because this was the most important hyperparameter in our preliminary experiments. Random walk is used to select new values of n with the step size being depended on the size of the domain, i.e., the number of observations and the number of sequences. Thus, when nR and nC were kept constant, the value of n was increased or decreased randomly based on the score $NDCG_5$ (Sec. 3), i.e., a form of coordinate ascent was performed on n. After the highest score was achieved by tuning n, n was frozen, and the algorithm used the same randomised procedure to tune nR. Finally, the same procedure was executed to tune the parameter nC.

On some problems, increasing n, nR and nC to large values was not possible as the algorithm became intractable.

5 Neural Models

Theoretically a single-layer RNN network should be able to approximate any computable function. However, it was observed recently that *empirically* multilayer deep RNNs work better than shallower (single layer) ones on some tasks, specifically on natural language processing tasks. For instance, Zaremba et al. (2014) used a stack of Long Short-Term Memory (LSTM) layers for language modelling and in (Sutskever et al., 2014) a 4-layer deep architecture was crucial in achieving good machine translation performance in an encoder-decoder framework. Apart from considering the number of layers as a hyperparameter, most recent works do not explain the advantage of multilayer RNNs. Moreover, the deep RNN language model (Zaremba et al., 2014) is used by numerous other models including Press and Wolf (2016); Gal and Ghahramani (2016). This was also used as a baseline in the exhaustive (over ten thousand different RNN architectures) architecture search by Jozefowicz et al. (2015) in pursuit of a better architecture, and they did not find architectures that were significantly better than the baselines. Therefore, a two-layer RNN is a strong baseline architecture for certain sequence prediction tasks, especially language modelling, where single-layer RNNs are not so powerful.

In the SPiCe competition, there were three neural models explored by Shibata and Heinz (2017) that achieved the winning accuracy. Among those models, the basic model is a two-layer stacked LSTM network. There is an all-connected non-linear layer with a Rectified Linear Unit (ReLU) activation function used on top of a stacked LSTM (Fig. 1a). The two-layer LSTM stack was placed on top of the embedding layer that is used to embed each symbol x_t of the sequence at position t. The output layer consists of a softmax layer implementing the softmax activation, which outputs the network's prediction of the next symbol of sequence $y_t = x_{t+1}$.

In this paper, we have simplified the basic architecture in two ways. First, we removed the fully-connected non-linear layer and introduced dropout to all non-recurrent layers (Fig. 1b). Second, we further simplified the model by using just a single layer (Fig. 1c) with dropout at non-recurrent layer. Dropout is an effective regularisation technique for deep neural networks (Hinton et al., 2012). The motivation for removing the all-connected layer is to reduce the number of parameters and the state-of-the-art sequence prediction models (Zaremba et al., 2014) do not usually have an all-connected non-linear layer on top of the stacked LSTM. Stacked LSTMs are expressive enough to capture most of regularities without an additional all-connected non-linear layer. The motivation for applying dropout to all non-recurrent layers is to regularise the whole networks (Zaremba et al., 2014) instead of regularising based on some particular layers (Shibata and Heinz, 2017). We compare against a single-layer LSTM in the results section.

Following Shibata and Heinz (2017) a 'start' symbol and an 'end' symbol were added to both sides of each training sentence. Symbols are fed into the model from the 'start' symbol.

5.1 Relevant Parameters and Parameter Search

Neural models have more hyperparameters than the other models (e.g. WFA). We used the hyperparameters from the baseline work (Shibata and Heinz, 2017) with two major exceptions: we used an LSTM network with one layer and two layers (contrary to the baseline work, we removed fully

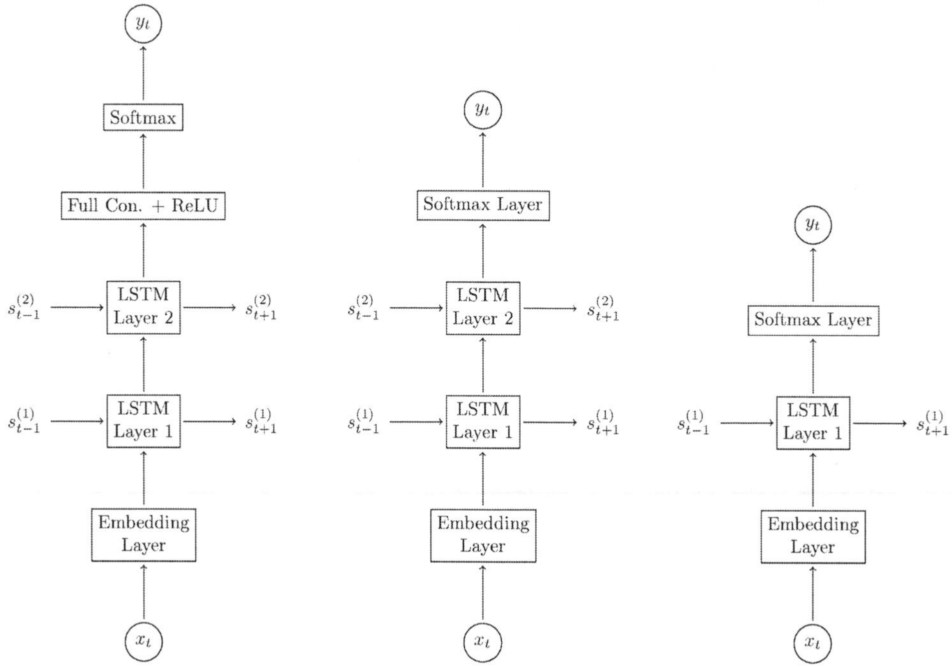

(a) Basic architecture (SPiCe) (b) Basic architecture (2-layer) (c) Basic architecture (1-layer)

Figure 1: Neural architectures for our experiments

connected layer as shown in Fig. 1b) and we applied the regularisation (i.e. dropout) differently than the baseline study. We applied dropout to regularise the whole network (except the recurrent layer) instead of just the last two layers (in baseline). The exact values of different parameters can be found in Sec. 6.

6 Experiments

The hyperparameters (see Tab. 1) for the WFA were tuned based on the approach described in Sec. 4.1 to find the best results obtained in this paper.

For the neural models, the weights were initialised with Gaussian samples, each of which has zero mean and standard deviation $\sqrt{\frac{1}{in\_size}}$, where in_size is the dimension of input vectors. The LSTM has 600 hidden nodes, the size of the embedding layer was set to 100, and when a non-linear layer is used between the LSTM and Softmax layers (for the baseline replication), the output dimension was set to 300. These values were set based on the baseline study (Shibata and Heinz, 2017), in which two hidden layer sizes (400 and 600) were used. In Shibata and Heinz (2017, Tables 1 and 2), hidden layer size did not have critical effect on the results. Considering SPiCe'16 datasets and the existing literature, 600 hidden nodes make a large RNN network. We have used two-layer and one-layer LSTM networks in our experiments. The dropout rate was set to 0.5 for all non-recurrent layers, which is known to be close to optimal for a wide range of networks and tasks (Srivastava et al., 2014).

Following the baseline study, for optimisation, we used stochastic gradient descent (SGD) with momentum of 0.9. The learning rate decreased gradually from 0.1 to 0.001, where the number of iterations is 45 and the mini-batch size is 128.

7 Results and Analysis

The main goal of our empirical investigation is to show that correlating the impact of multiple layers in RNN-based neural models with the number of hidden states (quantified using a rank of the SVD) in finite-state automata, we can increase the understanding of the deep neural networks. This way we aim to explain the role of multiple RNN layers in sequence modelling. In this discussion, we will refer to Tab. 1 that reports the scores of the three neural network models described in Sec. 5 and the scores of the WFA models described in Sec. 4.

Data	WFA				Neural Models (NN)			RNN Improv.
#	n	nR	nC	WFA	SPiCe NN	RNN (2 Layers)	RNN (1 Layer)	Gain in score
1	4	5	5	0.8789	0.909	**0.9180**	0.8521	0.0391
2	6	5	5	0.8731	0.920	**0.9210**	0.9183	0.0479
3	5	10	3	0.8248	0.888	**0.8938**	0.8819	0.0690
4	500	5	5	0.5272	**0.619**	0.6131	0.6142	0.0918
5	450	5	5	0.5688	0.8100	**0.8107**	0.7988	0.2419
6	90	6	7	0.8096	0.863	**0.8690**	0.7815	0.0594
7	500	4	4	0.4474	**0.736**	0.7258	0.7176	0.2886
8	60	5	5	0.5426	0.645	**0.6614**	0.6521	0.1188
9	57	8	7	0.9324	0.962	**0.9674**	0.9546	0.0350
10	200	5	5	0.3623	**0.574**	0.5526	0.5604	0.2117
11	100	5	5	0.4147	0.520	**0.5535**	0.5412	0.1388
12	95	4	4	0.8113	0.799	**0.8508**	0.7116	0.0395
13	500	5	5	0.4990	0.592	**0.6007**	0.5357	0.1017
14	2	10	10	**0.4649**	0.350	0.3496	0.3616	-
15	3	6	6	**0.2899**	0.263	0.2655	0.2651	-

Table 1: The hyperparameters of WFA, the scores of WFA and neural models, and the score improvement by the best neural model compared to WFA

Table 1 shows that the proposed one-layer neural network model has achieved competitive results compared with the two-layer stacked network on many of the SPiCe datasets. The additional layer in a two-layer model improved the score most significantly on dataset 12, where the score improved from 0.711 to 0.851 (0.14 units). Another dataset where improvement was observed was dataset 6 where the score improved by 0.088 units. On datasets 1 and 13, the improvements were 0.065 and 0.065 units. In addition to those bigger improvements, a two-layer stacked RNN achieved slight improvement in score (≤ 0.02) on datasets 2, 3, 5, 7, 8, 9, 10, and 11. Still, a one-layer network did better than at least one of the two-layer networks (i.e. SPiCe and the one proposed in this paper) on datasets 4, 8, 10, and 11. Overall, we can see that a one-layer RNN would be a better choice for some of our datasets, although using multiple layers leads to better predictions on other datasets. This means that in order to gain deeper insight into the behaviour of the methods, it is useful to investigate individual datasets in detail and include WFA in our analysis. For this reason, to shed some light on the impact of multiple layers in RNNs, we will analyse datasets 12 and 5 in the subsequent paragraphs. The reason for this choice is that on dataset 12, the score improved significantly using two layers, whereas on dataset 5 a similar improvement was not observed.

Dataset 12 and High Rank The synthetic dataset 12 was the biggest and arguably the most challenging problem in SPiCe 2016. It was initially generated for another competition (PAutomaC) using the PAutomaC data generator (Verwer et al., 2014a). The best performing WFA scored 0.8113 on this dataset with $n = 95$ and $nR = nC = 4$. Although WFA is a Markov model[2] (i.e., a model that may require l-th order representation, which makes predictions based on l the most recent observations, to learn long-range dependencies (Bengio and Frasconi, 1995b; Hinton et al., 2001; Kakade et al., 2016)), on dataset 12, WFA was as good as the RNN models. Our one-layer neural model scored 0.7116 and the two-layer neural model improved the result to 0.8508. So, we can clearly see that on this large dataset, two layers improve the results. We argue that we can use WFA results to explain the improvement of our two-layer neural model. For that we will focus on the rank of WFA (i.e. parameter n) and the maximum length of substrings in its basis (i.e. nR and nC). To score high on dataset 12, WFA had to use 95 hidden states, which is a large number of hidden states for a traditional Baum-Welch algorithm (Siddiqi et al., 2007). This means that

[2]Note that WFA is a generalisation of a Markov model where the next state depends only on the current state (Penagarikano and Bordel, 2004); every Markov model can be represented as a WFA.

in order to solve this problem, a Markov model requires a relatively large number of states. This fact can explain why our two-layer neural model outperformed a single-layer model because the second LSTM layer increased the number of hidden states in the neural model. Moreover, the obtained WFA's score is based on short substrings (i.e. $nR = nC = 4$) in its basis. Therefore, it is fair to expect that dataset 12 does not have long-term dependencies since short substring statistics are sufficient to capture the data-generating distribution in this model. We believe that we can make this claim because our WFA with short substrings works very well on this data. All this means that dataset 12 requires a relatively large number of hidden states, but it does not have long-term dependencies. Our two-layer neural model is sufficient for such problems because two layers increase the number of hidden states, whereas the long-term dependencies are not an issue.

To support our discussion above, we should add that in (Rabusseau et al., 2018) the hidden units of the second-order RNN were shown to be related to the rank or the hidden states of WFA. Note that second-order and higher-order RNNs have their recurrence depth increased by explicit, higher-order multiplicative interactions between the hidden states at previous time steps and input at the current time step. It was shown that any function that can be computed by a linear second-order RNN (Giles et al., 1992) with n hidden units on sequences of one-hot vectors (i.e. canonical basis vectors) can be computed by a WFA with n states. A higher-order RNN has additional connections from multiple previous time steps whereas the classic RNN has connection from one previous time step only. Higher order RNNs allow a direct mapping to a finite-state machine (Giles et al., 1992; Omlin and Giles, 1996). However, a similar connection is not available for classic RNNs and WFA and more importantly for multilayer RNNs and WFA. Based on these theoretical results and our empirical investigation, we can conjecture that the improved score on dataset 12 by using two LSTM layers indicates that the multiple layers helped to model the hidden states more efficiently.

Low Rank To support our arguments about the rank (i.e. the number of hidden states) in our discussion about dataset 12, we can identify a complementary relationship in other results. In particular, when we consider all datasets on which WFA did well having a small rank (this is in contrast to dataset 12 which required a high rank for WFA), a two-layer network does not lead to significant improvement. This pattern can be seen on datasets 1, 2, and 3, and this complements our previous arguments about dataset 12.

Dataset 5 and Long Context Dataset 5 is a real dataset on which the best performing WFA model scored 0.568 with rank $n = 450$ and substring lengths $nR = nC = 5$. This dataset is large for spectral learning and increasing nR and nC above 5 made the method intractable. Our one-layer neural model scored 0.7988 and a two-layer model showed a small improvement scoring 0.8107. This means that on this dataset adding more layers did not change the score significantly. We will attempt to explain the lack of a big improvement of a two-layer neural model using our WFA results.

Dataset 5 corresponds to the NLP character language modelling benchmark from Penn Treebank (Marcus et al., 1993b). The other NLP datasets are 4, 8, 11, and 13. Similar to dataset 5, increasing the number of RNN layers did not significantly improve the score on those datasets. Most NLP data (including dataset 5) have long-term dependencies because there are many training examples of word agreements (with different long-range regularities) which span a large portion of a sentence (Brown and Hinton, 2001). WFA with discrete states have limited memory capacity which gets consumed by having to deal with all the intervening regularities in the sequence. We can clearly see this in our results because in our experiments on WFA, we have many hidden states ($n = 450$). We can see that a large number of hidden states was not sufficient to solve this problem using WFA when $nR = nC = 5$, i.e., when substrings are short. In order to capture long-term dependencies, our WFA would need to be trained on longer substrings (higher nR and nC), but this is infeasible to do on this large dataset because the method becomes intractable. This problem requires the learning algorithm to take care of the long-term context.

We can provide a theoretical justification as to why long substrings (i.e. prefixes and suffixes that define the basis of a Hankel matrix) can lead to a better model given a particular number of hidden states, n. Note that the number of hidden states n corresponds to the number of dimensions that are kept after the SVD of the Henkel matrix. This means that n most informative latent dimensions (i.e., those that carry the most variance) are used as hidden states. If, given a particular value of n, one model has better performance than another model, it means that it's best n dimensions capture more variance than the best n latent dimensions of the alternative model. This argument explains why one basis of a Hankel matrix can lead to a better model than another basis. Intuitively, it is also natural to expect that long substrings can lead to a better set of hidden states because they can capture longer interactions between input symbols, which should naturally lead to more informative hidden states. If it was computationally feasible to evaluate dataset 5 with larger substring lengths, we could investigate the spectral norm of the empirical Hankel matrix with the increasing length of substrings (i.e. nR, nC). This would shed some light on the quality of the first hidden state in compared models.

Theoretically, a one-layer RNN model can capture infinite context (Siegelmann and Sontag, 1991), but due to training difficulties (e.g. the vanishing gradient problem), the context capture capacity of RNNs is limited. Despite this difficulty, it was shown in the literature that RNNs can capture previous context of up to 200 tokens (Khandelwal et al., 2018). However, other researchers (Pascanu et al., 2014) argue that stacking RNN layers (like in our two-layer model) does not increase the capacity of the model to capture longer contexts. This means that our two-layer model cannot deal with long contexts even when we add more layers. Since WFA did not perform well on dataset 5 having short context and a large number of hidden states, we conjecture that this dataset requires a long context and for this reason two-layers in a neural model do not help. Our results are consistent with other results where long-term contexts are captured by the recurrent layer (Bengio and Frasconi, 1995a). According to the distributed hypothesis (Bengio et al., 2009) stacking multiple layers allows for learning distributed features but not for capturing long-term contexts. Consequently, we assume that the long-term contexts are more important for dataset 5 to make efficient prediction than the pure increase in the number of the hidden states across the space.

Theoretical Considerations The relationship between the number of types of hidden states (discrete, or distributed), long-term dependency and the sequence prediction has been explored by Hinton et al. (2001); Bengio and Frasconi (1995b). For example, the hidden state of a single HMM (a specific version of WFA) can only convey $\log_2 K$ bits of information about the recent history. Instead, if a generative model had a distributed hidden state representation (Williams and Hinton, 1991) consisting of M variables each with K alternative states, it could convey $M \log_2 K$ bits of information. This means that the information bottleneck scales linearly with the number of variables and only logarithmically with the number of alternative states of each variable (Hinton et al., 2001). However, the link between the hidden state modelling and the number of recurrent neural network layers had not been explored before. From this theoretical analysis, we can see that if we have access to a large dataset then increasing the number of layers helps in modelling the hidden states more accurately (as seen in dataset 12), but it does not have to help to capture long-term contexts (dataset 5). In the latter case, one has to use models with high recurrence depth (Zilly et al., 2017; Pascanu et al., 2013), but we leave their exploration for future work since in this paper we wanted to focus on traditional LSTM layers.

Conclusion

Recurrent Neural Networks (RNNs) are a powerful tool for sequence modelling. However, RNNs are non-linear models, which makes them difficult to analyse theoretically. In this paper, we empirically analysed two RNN models (single-layer and two-layer RNNs) to understand the impact of the additional LSTM layers. We used Weighted Finite-state Automata (WFA) trained using the Hankel-based spectral learning algorithm. Based on fifteen benchmark datasets from the SPiCe 2016 competition, our empirical analyses indicate that multiple layers in RNNs help learning distributed hidden states through improved hidden space modelling but have lesser impact on the ability to learn long-term dependencies.

Acknowledgement We thank the four anonymous reviewers for their insightful and professional comments.

References

2010. TYPO CORPUS. `http://luululu.com/tweet/`. [Online; accessed 05-Feb-2019].

Guy Avni and Orna Kupferman. 2015. Stochastization of weighted automata. In *MFCS (1)*, volume 9234 of *Lecture Notes in Computer Science*, pages 89–102. Springer.

Borja Balle, Xavier Carreras, Franco M Luque, and Ariadna Quattoni. 2014. Spectral learning of weighted automata. *Machine learning*, 96(1-2):33–63.

Borja Balle, Rémi Eyraud, Franco M Luque, Ariadna Quattoni, and Sicco Verwer. 2017. Results of the sequence prediction challenge (spice): a competition on learning the next symbol in a sequence. In *International Conference on Grammatical Inference*, pages 132–136.

Borja Balle, Ariadna Quattoni, and Xavier Carreras. 2012. Local loss optimization in operator models: A new insight into spectral learning. In *ICML*. icml.cc / Omnipress.

Yoshua Bengio and Paolo Frasconi. 1995a. Diffusion of context and credit information in markovian models. *Journal of Artificial Intelligence Research*, 3:249–270.

Yoshua Bengio and Paolo Frasconi. 1995b. Diffusion of credit in markovian models. In G. Tesauro, D. S. Touretzky, and T. K. Leen, editors, *Advances in Neural Information Processing Systems 7*, pages 553–560. MIT Press.

Yoshua Bengio et al. 2009. Learning deep architectures for ai. *Foundations and trends in Machine Learning*, 2(1):1–127.

Andrew D Brown and Geoffrey E Hinton. 2001. Products of hidden markov models. In *AISTATS*.

AJ Buchsbaum, Raffaele Giancarlo, and Jeffery R Westbrook. 1998. Shrinking language models by robust approximation. In *Proceedings of the 1998 IEEE International Conference on Acoustics, Speech and Signal Processing, ICASSP'98 (Cat. No. 98CH36181)*, volume 2, pages 685–688. IEEE.

Rafael C Carrasco and José Oncina. 1994. Learning stochastic regular grammars by means of a state merging method. In *International Colloquium on Grammatical Inference*, pages 139–152. Springer.

Olivier Delalleau and Yoshua Bengio. 2011. Shallow vs. deep sum-product networks. In *Advances in Neural Information Processing Systems*, pages 666–674.

Salah El Hihi and Yoshua Bengio. 1996. Hierarchical recurrent neural networks for long-term dependencies. In *Advances in neural information processing systems*, pages 493–499.

Jeffrey L. Elman. 1990. Finding structure in time. *COGNITIVE SCIENCE*, 14(2):179–211.

Robert D Finn, Penelope Coggill, Ruth Y Eberhardt, Sean R Eddy, Jaina Mistry, Alex L Mitchell, Simon C Potter, Marco Punta, Matloob Qureshi, Amaia Sangrador-Vegas, et al. 2015. The pfam protein families database: towards a more sustainable future. *Nucleic acids research*, 44(D1):D279–D285.

Yarin Gal and Zoubin Ghahramani. 2016. A theoretically grounded application of dropout in recurrent neural networks. In *Proc. of NIPS*, pages 1019–1027.

C. L. Giles, C. B. Miller, D. Chen, H. H. Chen, G. Z. Sun, and Y. C. Lee. 1992. Learning and extracting finite state automata with second-order recurrent neural networks. *Neural Comput.*, 4(3):393–405.

Ian J. Goodfellow, David Warde-Farley, Mehdi Mirza, Aaron Courville, and Yoshua Bengio. 2013. Maxout networks. In *Proceedings of the 30th International Conference on International Conference on Machine Learning - Volume 28*, ICML'13, pages III–1319–III–1327. JMLR.org.

GE Hinton, AD Brown, and Queen Square London. 2001. Training many small hidden markov models. *Proc. of the Workshop on Innovation in Speech Processing*.

Geoffrey E Hinton, Nitish Srivastava, Alex Krizhevsky, Ilya Sutskever, and Ruslan R Salakhutdinov. 2012. Improving neural networks by preventing co-adaptation of feature detectors. *arXiv preprint arXiv:1207.0580*.

Micah Hodosh, Peter Young, and Julia Hockenmaier. 2013. Framing image description as a ranking task: Data, models and evaluation metrics. *Journal of Artificial Intelligence Research*, 47:853–899.

Falk Howar, Malte Isberner, Maik Merten, Bernhard Steffen, Dirk Beyer, and Corina S. Pasareanu. 2014. Rigorous examination of reactive systems - the RERS challenges 2012 and 2013. *STTT*, 16(5):457–464.

Daniel Hsu, Sham M Kakade, and Tong Zhang. 2012. A spectral algorithm for learning hidden markov models. *Journal of Computer and System Sciences*, 78(5):1460–1480.

Rafal Jozefowicz, Wojciech Zaremba, and Ilya Sutskever. 2015. An empirical exploration of recurrent network architectures. In *International Conference on Machine Learning*, pages 2342–2350.

Sham M. Kakade, Percy Liang, Vatsal Sharan, and Gregory Valiant. 2016. Prediction with a short memory. *CoRR*, abs/1612.02526.

Urvashi Khandelwal, He He, Peng Qi, and Dan Jurafsky. 2018. Sharp nearby, fuzzy far away: How neural language models use context. In *Proceedings of the 56th Annual Meeting of the Association for Computational Linguistics (Volume 1: Long Papers)*, pages 284–294. Association for Computational Linguistics.

Hugo Larochelle, Dumitru Erhan, Aaron Courville, James Bergstra, and Yoshua Bengio. 2007. An empirical evaluation of deep architectures on problems with many factors of variation. In *Proceedings of the 24th international conference on Machine learning*, pages 473–480. ACM.

Nicolas Le Roux and Yoshua Bengio. 2010. Deep belief networks are compact universal approximators. *Neural computation*, 22(8):2192–2207.

Mitchell P. Marcus, Mary Ann Marcinkiewicz, and Beatrice Santorini. 1993a. Building a large annotated corpus of english: The penn treebank. *Comput. Linguist.*, 19(2):313–330.

Mitchell P Marcus, Mary Ann Marcinkiewicz, and Beatrice Santorini. 1993b. Building a large annotated corpus of english: The penn treebank. *Computational linguistics*, 19(2):313–330.

Mehryar Mohri. 2004. Weighted finite-state transducer algorithms. an overview. In *Formal Languages and Applications*, pages 551–563. Springer.

Christian W Omlin and C Lee Giles. 1996. Constructing deterministic finite-state automata in recurrent neural networks. *Journal of the ACM (JACM)*, 43(6):937–972.

Razvan Pascanu, Çaglar Gülçehre, Kyunghyun Cho, and Yoshua Bengio. 2014. How to construct deep recurrent neural networks. *In the Proc. of ICLR*.

Razvan Pascanu, Guido Montufar, and Yoshua Bengio. 2013. On the number of response regions of deep feed forward networks with piece-wise linear activations. *arXiv preprint arXiv:1312.6098*.

Mikel Penagarikano and German Bordel. 2004. Layered Markov models: a new architectural approach to automatic speech recognition. In *Proceedings of the 2004 14th IEEE Signal Processing Society Workshop Machine Learning for Signal Processing, 2004.*, pages 305–314. IEEE.

Ofir Press and Lior Wolf. 2016. Using the output embedding to improve language models. *In the Proc. of EACL*, 2:157–163.

Guillaume Rabusseau, Tianyu Li, and Doina Precup. 2018. Connecting weighted automata and recurrent neural networks through spectral learning. *arXiv preprint arXiv:1807.01406*.

Jürgen Schmidhuber. 2008. Learning complex, extended sequences using the principle of history compression. *Learning*, 4(2).

Vatsal Sharan, Sham M Kakade, Percy S Liang, and Gregory Valiant. 2017. Learning overcomplete hmms. In *Advances in Neural Information Processing Systems*, pages 940–949.

Chihiro Shibata and Jeffrey Heinz. 2017. Predicting sequential data with lstms augmented with strictly 2-piecewise input vectors. In *International Conference on Grammatical Inference*, pages 137–142.

Sajid M Siddiqi, Geogrey J Gordon, and Andrew W Moore. 2007. Fast state discovery for hmm model selection and learning. In *Artificial Intelligence and Statistics*, pages 492–499.

Hava T. Siegelmann and Eduardo D. Sontag. 1991. Turing computability with neural nets. *Applied Mathematics Letters*, 4:77–80.

Nitish Srivastava, Geoffrey E Hinton, Alex Krizhevsky, Ilya Sutskever, and Ruslan Salakhutdinov. 2014. Dropout: a simple way to prevent neural networks from overfitting. *Journal of Machine Learning Research*, 15(1):1929–1958.

Ilya Sutskever, Oriol Vinyals, and Quoc V Le. 2014. Sequence to sequence learning with neural networks. In *Advances in neural information processing systems*, pages 3104–3112.

Mariona Taulé, Maria Antònia Martí, and Marta Recasens. 2008. Ancora: Multilevel annotated corpora for Catalan and Spanish. In *LREC*. European Language Resources Association.

Sicco Verwer, Rémi Eyraud, and Colin De La Higuera. 2014a. Pautomac: a probabilistic automata and hidden markov models learning competition. *Machine learning*, 96(1-2):129–154.

Sicco Verwer, Rémi Eyraud, and Colin dela Higuera. 2014b. Pautomac: a probabilistic automata and hidden markov models learning competition. *Machine Learning*, 96(1):129–154.

Christopher KI Williams and Geoffrey E Hinton. 1991. Mean field networks that learn to discriminate temporally distorted strings. In *Connectionist Models*, pages 18–22. Elsevier.

Wojciech Zaremba, Ilya Sutskever, and Oriol Vinyals. 2014. Recurrent neural network regularization. *arXiv preprint arXiv:1409.2329*.

Julian Georg Zilly, Rupesh Kumar Srivastava, Jan Koutník, and Jürgen Schmidhuber. 2017. Recurrent highway networks. In *Proceedings of the 34th International Conference on Machine Learning-Volume 70*, pages 4189–4198. JMLR. org.

Multi-Element Long Distance Dependencies: Using SPk Languages to Explore the Characteristics of Long-Distance Dependencies

Abhijit Mahalunkar
Applied Intelligence Research Center
Technological University Dublin
Dublin, Ireland
abhijit.mahalunkar@mydit.ie

John D. Kelleher
ADAPT Research Center
Technological University Dublin
Dublin, Ireland
john.d.kelleher@dit.ie

Abstract

In order to successfully model Long Distance Dependencies (LDDs) it is necessary to understand the full-range of the characteristics of the LDDs exhibited in a target dataset. In this paper, we use Strictly k-Piecewise languages to generate datasets with various properties. We then compute the characteristics of the LDDs in these datasets using mutual information and analyze the impact of factors such as (i) k, (ii) length of LDDs, (iii) vocabulary size, (iv) forbidden subsequences, and (v) dataset size. This analysis reveal that the number of interacting elements in a dependency is an important characteristic of LDDs. This leads us to the challenge of modelling multi-element long-distance dependencies. Our results suggest that attention mechanisms in neural networks may aide in modeling datasets with multi-element long-distance dependencies. However, we conclude that there is a need to develop more efficient attention mechanisms to address this issue.

1 Introduction

Long Distance Dependencies (LDDs) describe an interaction between two (or more) elements in a sequence that are separated by an arbitrary number of positions. LDDs are related to the rate of decay of statistical dependence of two points with increasing time interval or spatial distance between them. For example, in English there is a requirement for subjects and verbs to agree, compare: "*The* ***dog*** *in that house* ***is*** *aggressive*" with "*The* ***dogs*** *in that house* ***are*** *aggressive*". This dependence can be computed using information theoretic measure i.e. *Mutual Information* (Cover and Thomas, 1991; Paninski, 2003; Bouma, 2009; Lin and Tegmark, 2017).

To date most research on LDDs has focused on the distance the dependency spans within the sequence. However, as our analysis will show the complexity of LDDs not only arises from the distance but also a number of other factors, including: (i) the number of unique symbols in a dataset, (ii) the size of the dataset, (iii) the number of interacting symbols within an LDD, and (iv) the distance between the interacting symbols. In this paper we use SPk languages to explore the complexity of LDDs. The motivation for using the SPk language modelling task, is that the standard sequential benchmark datasets provide little to no control over the factors which directly contribute to LDD characteristics. By contrast, using SPk languages we can generate benchmark datasets with varying degrees of LDD complexity by modifying the grammar of the SPk language (Rogers et al., 2010; Fu et al., 2011; Avcu et al., 2017).

One aspect of LDDs that has been neglected in the research on LDDs is the complexity that arises from a multi-element dependency (i.e., dependencies that involves interactions between more than 2 elements). By controlling k in the SPk grammar, it is possible to generate datasets with varying degrees of multi-element dependency. This multi-element dependencies pose specific challenges to neural architectures that may require these architectures to be augmented with pointer or attention mechanisms. We explore whether attention mechanism can help with multi-element LDDs using two models, Transformer-XL (Dai* et al., 2019) and AWD-LSTM (Merity et al., 2018). Transformer-XL employs multi-head attention mechanism along with recurrence mechanism. Whereas, AWD-LSTM is a weight dropped LSTM which does not employ any attention/pointer mechanism.

The Transformer-XL and AWD-LSTM models are both *language models*. A language model accepts a sequence of symbols and predicts the next symbol in the sequence. The accuracy of a language model is dependent on the capacity of the

Proceedings of the Workshop on Deep Learning and Formal Languages: Building Bridges, pages 34–43
Florence, Italy, August, 2nd 2019.

model to capture the LDDs in the data on which it is evaluated. The standard evaluation metric for language models is *perplexity*. Perplexity is the measurement of the confusion or uncertainty of a language model as it predicts the next symbol in a sequence, and the lower the perplexity of a model the better the performance of the model.

2 Related Work: Neural Networks and Artificial Grammars

Formal Language Theory, primarily developed to study the computational basis of human language is now being used extensively to analyze any rule-governed system (Chomsky, 1956, 1959; Fitch and Friederici, 2012). Formal languages have previously been used to train RNNs and investigate their inner workings. The Reber grammar (Reber, 1967) was used to train various 1st order RNNs (Casey, 1996; Smith and Zipser, 1989). The Reber grammar was also used as a benchmarking dataset for LSTM models (Hochreiter and Schmidhuber, 1997). Regular languages, studied by Tomita (Tomita, 1982), were used to train 2nd order RNNs to learn grammatical structures of the strings (Watrous and Kuhn, 1991; Giles et al., 1992).

Regular languages are the simplest grammars (type-3 grammars) within the Chomsky hierarchy which are driven by regular expressions. For neural network research an interesting subclass of regular languages is the Strictly k-Piecewise languages. Strictly k-Piecewise languages are natural and can express some of the kinds of LDDs found in natural languages (Jager and Rogers, 2012; Heinz and Rogers, 2010). This presents an opportunity of using SPk grammar to generate benchmarking datasets (Avcu et al., 2017; Mahalunkar and Kelleher, 2018). In Avcu et al. (2017), LSTM networks were trained to recognize valid strings generated using SP2, SP4, SP8 grammar. LSTM could recognize valid strings generated using SP2 and SP4 grammars but struggled to recognize strings generated using SP8 grammar, exposing the performance bottleneck of LSTM networks. It has also been observed that the performance of LSTMs on SP2 datasets degraded when the length of the LDDs in the datasets were increased, this was done by increasing the maximum length of the generated strings of SP2 (Mahalunkar and Kelleher, 2018).

3 Preliminaries

3.1 Strictly k-Piecewise Languages (SPk)

SPk languages form a subclass of regular languages. Subregular languages can be identified by mechanisms much less complicated than Finite-State Automata. Many aspects of human language such as local and non-local dependencies are similar to subregular languages (Jager and Rogers, 2012). More importantly, there are certain types of long distance (non-local) dependencies in human language which allow finite-state characterization (Heinz and Rogers, 2010). These type of LDDs can easily be characterized by SPk languages and can be easily extended to other processes.

A language L, is described by a finite set of unique symbols Σ and Σ^* (*free monoid*) is a set of finite sequences or strings of zero or more elements from Σ.

Example 3.1. Consider, $\Sigma = \{\sigma_1, \sigma_2, \sigma_3, \sigma_4\}$ where $\sigma_1, \sigma_2, \sigma_3, \sigma_4$ are the unique symbols. A *free monoid* over Σ contains all concatenations of these unique symbols. Thus, $\Sigma^* = \{\lambda, \sigma_1, \sigma_1\sigma_2, \sigma_1\sigma_3, \sigma_1\sigma_4, \sigma_3\sigma_2, \sigma_3\sigma_1\sigma_3, \sigma_2\sigma_1\sigma_4\sigma_3, ... \}$.

Definition 3.1. Let, u denote a string, e.g. $u = \sigma_3\sigma_2$. The length of a string u is denoted by $|u|$, and if $u = \sigma_3\sigma_2$ then $|u|=2$. A string with length zero is denoted by λ.

Definition 3.2. A string v is a *subsequence* of string w, iff $v = \sigma_1\sigma_2 ... \sigma_n$ and $w \in \Sigma^*\sigma_1\Sigma^*\sigma_2\Sigma^* ... \Sigma^*\sigma_n\Sigma^*$, where $\sigma \in \Sigma$. A *subsequence* of length k is called a *k-subsequence*. Let $\text{subseq}_k(w)$ denote the set of subsequences of w up to length k.

Example 3.2. Consider, $\Sigma = \{a, b, c, d\}$, $w = [acbd]$, $u = [bd]$, $v = [acd]$ and $x = [db]$. String u is a *subsequence* of length $k = 2$ or *2-subsequence* of w. String v is a *3-subsequence* of w. However, string x is *not a subsequence* of w as it does not contain $[db]$ subsequence.

SPk languages are defined by grammar G_{SPk} as a set of permissible *k-subsequences*. Here, k indicates the number of elements in a dependency. Datasets generated to simulate 2 elements in a dependency will be generated using SP2. This is the simplest dependency structure. There are more complex chained-dependency structures which require higher k grammars.

Example 3.3. Consider L, where $\Sigma = \{a, b, c, d\}$. Let G_{SP2} be SPk grammar which is comprised of permissible *2-subsequences*. Thus, $G_{SP2} = \{aa,$

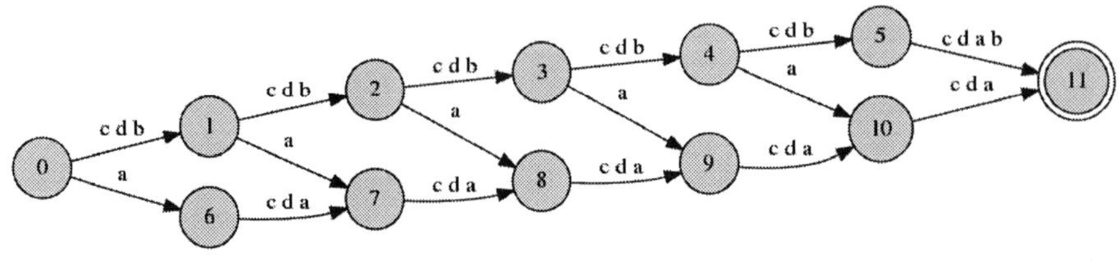

Figure 1: The automaton for G_{SP2} where n_l=6

ac, ad, ba, bb, bc, bd, ca, cb, cc, cd, da, db, dc, dd}. G_{SP2} grammar is employed to generate SP2 datasets.

Definition 3.3. Subsequences which are not in the grammar *G* are called *forbidden subsequences*[1].

Example 3.4. Consider Example 3.3, although $\{ab\}$ is a possible *2-subsequence*, it is not part of the grammar G_{SP2}. Hence, $\{ab\}$ is a *forbidden subsequence*.

Example 3.5. Consider strings *u, v, w*: *u* = [*bbcbdd*], *v* = [*bbdbbbcbddaa*] and *w* = [*bbabbbcbdd*], where $|u| = 6$, $|v| = 12$ and $|w| = 10$. Strings *u* and *v* are valid SP2 strings because they are composed of subsequences that are in G_{SP2}. However, *w* is an invalid SP2 string because *w* contains $\{ab\}$ a subsequence which is a *forbidden subsequence*. These constraints apply for any string *x* where $|x| \in \mathbb{Z}$.

Example 3.6. Let G_{SP3} = {*aaa, aab, abb, baa, bab, bba, bbb, ...*} and *forbidden subsequence* = {*aba*} be an SP*3* grammar which is comprised of permissible *3-subsequences*. Thus, *u* = [*aaaaaaab*], where $|u| = 8$ is a valid SP*3* string and *v* = [*aaaaabaab*], where $|v| = 9$ is an invalid SP*3* string as defined by the grammar G_{SP3}.

The maximum extent of LDD exhibited by a certain SP*k* language is equal to the length of the strings generated which abide by the grammar. However, as per definition 3.2, the strings generated using this method will also exhibit dependencies of shorter lengths. It should be noted that the length of the LDD is not the same as *k*. The length of the LDD is the maximum distance between two elements in a dependency, whereas *k* specifies the number of elements in the dependency (as defined in the the SP*k* grammar).

Example 3.7. As per Example 3.5, *v* = [*bbdbbbcbddaa*], consider *b* in the first position, *subsequence* {*ba*} exhibits dependency of 10 and 11. Similarly, *subsequence* {*bd*} exhibits dependency of 2, 9, 10, etc.

Figure 1 depicts a finite-state diagram of G_{SP2}, which generates strings of synthetic data. Consider a string *x* from this data, $\forall$ generated strings *x* generated using grammar G_{SP2}: $|x| = 6$. The *forbidden subsequence* for this grammar is $\{ab\}$. Since $\{ab\}$ is a *forbidden subsequence*, the state diagram has no path (from state 0 to state 11) because such a path would permit the generation of strings with $\{ab\}$ as a subsequence, *e.g.* {*abcccc*} Traversing the state diagram generates valid strings *e.g.* {*accdda, caaaaa*}.

Various G_{SPk} could be used to define an SP*k* depending on the set of *forbidden subsequences* chosen. Thus, we can construct rich datasets with different properties for any SP*k* language. *forbidden subsequences* allow for the elimination of certain logically possible sequences while simulating a real world dataset where the probability of occurrence of that particular sequence is highly unlikely. Every SP*k* grammar is defined with at least one *forbidden subsequence.*

3.2 Plotting LDD Characteristics

Mutual information has previously been used to analyse LDDs in datasets. For example, in Ebeling and Poeschel (2002), mutual information was used to analyse the maximum length of the LDDs in two English literary texts, Moby Dick by H. Melville and Grimm's tales. Another example, is the work of Lin and Tegmark (2017) who analyzed the LDD characteristics in *enwik8* dataset.

Mutual information measures dependence between random variables X and Y. These random variables have marginal distributions $p(x)$ and $p(y)$ and are jointly distributed as $p(x, y)$ (Cover and Thomas, 1991; Li, 1990). Mutual information, $I(X;Y)$ is defined as;

$$I(X;Y) = \sum_{x,y} p(x,y) \log \frac{p(x,y)}{p(x)p(y)} \quad (1)$$

[1] Refer section *5.2. Finding the shortest forbidden subsequences* in (Fu et al., 2011) for method to compute *forbidden sequences* for SP*k* language

If X and Y are not correlated, in other words if they are independent to each other, then $p(x)p(y) = p(x, y)$ and $I(X;Y) = 0$. However, if X and Y are fully dependent on each other, then $p(x) = p(y) = p(x, y)$ which results in the maximum value of $I(X;Y)$.

Mutual information can also be expressed using the *entropy* of X and Y i.e. $H(X)$, $H(Y)$ and their *joint entropy*, $H(X, Y)$ as given in the equations below:

$$I(X;Y) = H(X) + H(Y) - H(X,Y) \quad (2)$$

$$H(X) = -\sum_{x} p(x) \log p(x) \quad (3)$$

In our algorithm, we compute the $H(X)$ using Grassberger's corrections (Grassberger, 2003).

$$H(X) = \log N - 1/N \sum_{i=1}^{k} N_i \psi(N_i) \quad (4)$$

where N_i is the frequency of unique symbol i, $N = \sum N_i$, K is the number of unique symbols, and $\psi(N_i)$ is the *logarithmic derivative of the gamma function* of N_i.

In order to measure dependence between any two symbols at a distance D in a sequence, we design random variables X and Y so that X holds the subsequence of the original sequence from index 0 till $|dataset| - 1 - D$, and Y holds the subsequence from index D till $|dataset| - 1$; where D represents spacing between the symbols and $|dataset|$ or LEN is the size of the dataset. Next we define a random variable XY that contains a sequence of paired symbols one from X and one from Y, where the symbols in a pair have the same index in X and Y. Algorithm 1 explains the details.

Using this information, and Equations 2 and 4, we calculate the mutual information $I(X, Y)$ at a distance D in a sequence. We define the *LDD characteristics* of any given sequential dataset as a function of mutual information $I(X;Y)$ over the distance D. Once we have calculated the mutual information within a dataset at the different distances D which range between 1 to $|dataset|$ we can then plot the LDD characteristics as a graph of distance D versus mutual information at D. The LDD characteristics are plotted on a *log-log axis*, the *x-axis* defines the distance between a pair of symbols and the *y-axis* marks the mutual information.

Algorithm 1 Computing LDD Characteristics

```
for D ← 1, |dataset| do
    X ← dataset[0 : |dataset| − D]
    Y ← dataset[D : |dataset|]
    XY ← zero-matrix of size (K^X, K^Y)
    for i ← 0, |X| do
        Increment XY[X[i], Y[i]]
    end for
    Compute N_i^X, N^X, K^X for X
    Compute N_i^Y, N^Y, K^Y for Y
    Compute N_i^XY, N^XY, K^XY for XY
    Compute H(X), H(Y) and H(X,Y) Eq. 4
    I[D] ← H(X) + H(Y) − H(X,Y)
end for
```

4 LDD characteristics of SP*k* datasets

Natural datasets present little to no control over the factors that affect LDDs. This, limits our ability to understand LDDs in more detail. SP*k* languages exhibit some types of LDDs occurring in natural datasets. Moreover, by modifying the SP*k* grammar we can control the LDD characteristics within a dataset generated by the grammar. To understand and validate the interaction between an SP*k* grammar and the characteristics of the data it generates, we used a number of datasets of SP*k* grammar and analyzed the properties of these datasets. Every dataset is a collection of strings and these strings strictly follow the grammar. Hence the size of the dataset ($|dataset|$) is the sum of the size of all the strings. The datasets were generated using *foma* (Hulden, 2009) and *python* (Avcu et al., 2017; Mahalunkar and Kelleher, 2018)[2]. Below we analyze the impact of various factors on the resulting LDD characteristics.

4.1 Impact of *k*

A dependency may arise within a dataset due to two or more interacting elements. A two element dependency is the simplest dependency structure and is analyzed by models addressing LDDs. However, multiple element dependency may not be rare and if not modeled correctly may well contribute to the errors of a model. Lack of knowledge of these dependency structures within benchmark datasets present significant limitation in comparing the performance of different models aimed at addressing LDDs. Different model architectures

[2]The scripts and details of these datasets are available at `https://github.com/silentknight/DelFol-ACL-2019`

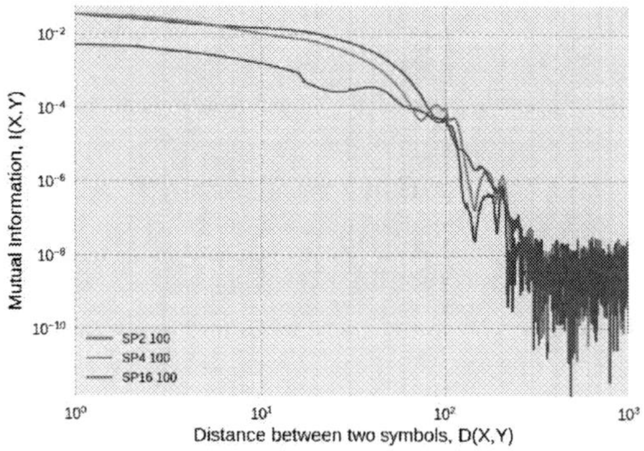

Figure 2: LDD characteristics of datasets of SP2, SP*4* and SP*16* grammar exhibiting LDD of length 100.

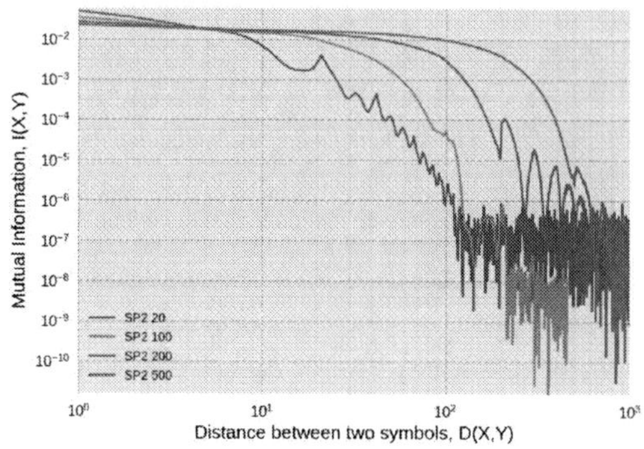

Figure 3: LDD characteristics of datasets of SP*2* grammar exhibiting LDDs of length 20, 100, 200 and 500.

may be able to represent one type of LDD characteristic to a greater extent than another (e.g., distance versus k). However, unless the experimenter is able to control the LDD characteristics present in a dataset it is not possible to disentangle which characteristics a given model struggles with based solely on the models performance on the data. SP*k* grammar addresses this problem by providing control over both dependency distance and k.

We use SP*2*, SP*4* and SP*16* grammars to generate a set of datasets. With k=$\{2, 4, 16\}$, we generate datasets with different dependency structures with interacting elements $2, 4$, and 16 respectively. Figure 2 plots the LDD characteristics of SP*2*, SP*4* and SP*16* grammars. They contain uniform distribution of strings of string length l where $60 \leq l \leq 100$. The maximum length of strings in each of these datasets is 100. Hence, we can observe steeper mutual information decay beyond $D > 100$. k defines the number of correlated or dependent elements in a dependency rule. As k increases the grammar becomes more complex and there is an overall reduction in frequency of the dependent elements in a given sequence (due to lower probability of these elements occurring in a given sequence). Hence, the mutual information is lower. This can be seen with dataset of SP*16* as compared to SP*2* and SP*4*. It is worth noting that datasets with lower mutual information curves tend to present more difficulty during modeling (Mahalunkar and Kelleher, 2018).

4.2 Impact of LDD length

The distance or length between two interacting elements present significant challenge in modeling LDDs as the model is required to store the context of the interacting element persistently. The success of a model is dependent on whether it is capable of storing the required length of the contexts as dictated by the dataset.

We generated strings of maximum length 20 $(2 \leq l \leq 20)$, 100 $(21 \leq l \leq 100)$, 200 $(101 \leq l \leq 200)$ and 500 $(201 \leq l \leq 500)$ using SP*2* grammar. As explained in Example 3.6, by increasing the length of the generated strings, the distance between dependent elements is also increased, resulting in longer LDDs. Consequently, using this string lengths we can simulate LDD lengths of $20, 100, 200$ and 500.

Figure 3 plots LDD characteristics of SP2 languages with maximum string length of $20, 100, 200, 500$. The point where mutual information decay is faster, the *inflection point*, lies around the same point on *x-axis* as the maximum length of the LDD. This confirms that SP*k* can generate datasets with varying lengths of LDDs.

4.3 Impact of Vocabulary Size

We analyze the impact of vocabulary size on LDD characteristics, we generate SP2 grammars where Σ_1=$\{a, b, c, d\}$ (V=4) and Σ_2=$\{a, b, c, d, ..., x, y, z\}$ (V=26), where V is vocabulary size. The impact of vocabulary size can be seen in figure 4. Both these datasets contain strings of maximum length 20. Hence the mutual information decays at 20. Both curves have identical decay indicating a similar grammar. However the overall mutual information of the dataset with V=26 is much lower then the mutual information of the dataset with V=4. This is because a smaller vocabulary results in an increase in the probability of the occurrence of each individual elements.

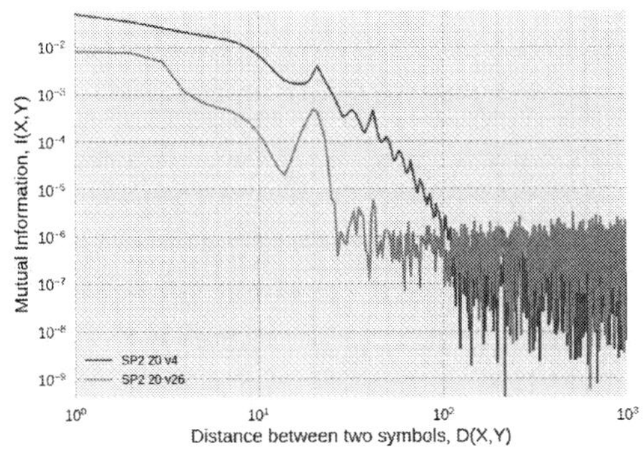

Figure 4: LDD characteristics of datasets of SP2 grammar with vocabulary of 4 and 26.

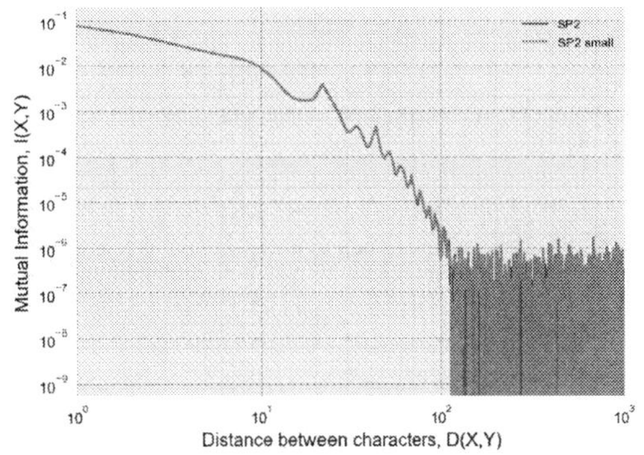

Figure 6: LDD characteristics of datasets of SP2 grammar with varying size of the datasets

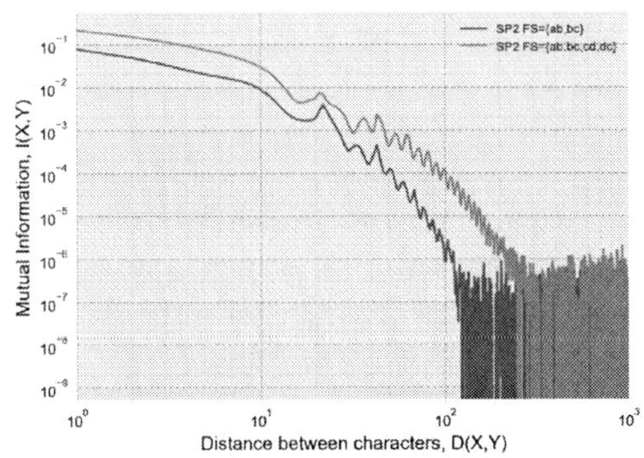

Figure 5: LDD characteristics of datasets of SP2 grammar with varying forbidden subsequences.

4.4 Impact of *forbidden subsequences*

forbidden subsequences control the complexity of a given grammar. We choose two sets of forbidden subsequences for SP2 grammar, $\{ab, bc\}$ and $\{ab, bc, cd, dc\}$.

Figure 5 plots the LDD characteristics of SP2 grammar with two set of *forbidden subsequences* as $\{ab, bc\}$ and $\{ab, bc, cd, dc\}$. It is seen that the dataset with more forbidden subsequences exhibited mutual information decay tending towards a power law decay as compared to an exponential decay by dataset with less forbidden subsequences. As explained in Lin and Tegmark (2017), datasets with exponential decay tend to exhibit Markovian behavior and thus are easy to model as compared to datasets with power law decay. Complex LDDs in a dataset result in power law decay. Thus, by controlling the forbidden subsequences, one can introduce more complex LDDs.

4.5 Impact of dataset size

Another factor to analyze is the impact of the size of the dataset ($|dataset|$) on LDDs of the same grammar. We generate two sizes of the same SP2 grammar to study the impact of the size of the data on the LDD characteristics, where one dataset is twice the size of the other.

In figure 6 we can observe that LDD characteristics of datasets sampled from the same grammar are less likely to be affected by the size of the dataset.

5 Multi-Element Long Distance Dependencies: Attention Mechanisms and *k*

As discussed above in section 4.1, LDDs may arise due to multiple interacting elements, which can be referred to as multi-element long-distance dependency (ME-LDD). Current LDD research primarily focuses on developing models which are capable of retaining contextual information across long distances in sequential datasets. This approach, which focuses solely on dependency distance, may be insufficient in addressing the problems arising due to ME-LDDs. However, recent advances in attention mechanisms and memory networks may be able to represent ME-LDDs. In this section we investigate two models, Transformer-XL (Dai* et al., 2019) (with attention mechanism) and AWD-LSTM (ASGD Weight-Dropped LSTM) (without attention mechanism) (Merity et al., 2018) so as to analyze how attention mechanisms help in modeling datasets with ME-LDDs.

The Transformer-XL model augments vanilla Transformer models by introducing a recurrence mechanism to the Transformer architecture. This recurrence effectively encodes an arbitrarily long context into a fixed size representation over constrained memory and computation. A vanilla Transformer is made up of Multi-Head Attention

Models	Test Perplexity in *bpc*			
	SP2	SP4	SP8	SP16
1	1.6855	1.8038	1.9611	2.0759
2	1.413	1.486	1.658	1.708

Table 1: Perplexity score of 1: Transformer-XL and 2: AWD-LSTM models of SP2, SP4, SP8 and SP16 datasets with vocabulary size V=4

Models	Test Perplexity in *bpc*			
	SP2	SP4	SP6	SP8
1	4.6846	4.7320	4.7384	4.7385
2	4.525	4.635	4.707	4.708

Table 2: Perplexity score of 1: Transformer-XL and 2: AWD-LSTM models of SP2, SP4, SP6 and SP8 datasets with vocabulary size V=26

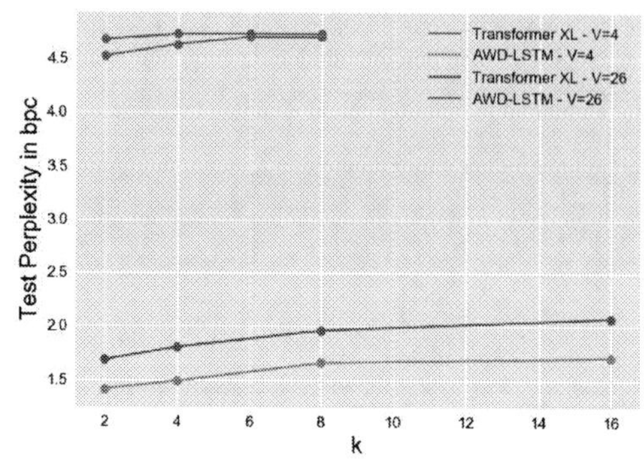

Figure 7: Test perplexity score of Transformer-XL and AWD-LSTM models of SP2, SP4, SP8 and SP16 datasets.

and Feed Forward layers which aides in adding positional information to the embedded representation. The other model we tested, the AWD-LSTM, uses a weight-drop mechanism so as to aid in regularization of the LSTM network. Hence this model does not explicitly uses attention mechanism.

We trained both these models with variants of SPk grammar where k=$\{2, 4, 8, 16\}$ for vocabulary size V=4 and k=$\{2, 4, 6, 8\}$ for vocabulary size V=26. Hence, there are in total 8 datasets. Every dataset contains uniform distribution of strings with string length l where $60 \leq l \leq 100$. The string length ordering is not maintained so as to not bias the models. In-order to train the language models, every dataset is split into training/validation/test sets. All the training sets for vocabulary size V=4 contain $\approx$195000 number of strings and the size of the training set is $\approx 24MB$. Similarly, all the training sets for vocabulary size V=26 contain $\approx$222000 number of strings with size of $\approx 40MB$. All the test and validation sets contain $\approx$16000 strings with size of $2MB$[3]. The hyperparameters for both the models were reused from the *Penn Treebank character* model (Dai* et al., 2019; Merity et al., 2018).

Table 1 lists the test perplexity scores of both the models in *bits per character* for datasets with vocabulary size V=4 and table 2 lists the test perplexity scores of both the models for datasets with vocabulary size V=26. We plot the test perplexity scores of all the datasets as function of k in figure 7. Here we observe two distinct sets of perplexity growth curves. It can be seen that, as the size of the vocabulary changes, the test perplexity score across all the models also changes relatively. This confirms that the vocabulary size of the dataset does impact the perplexity score of the models. This is attributed to the lower mutual information in the LDD characteristics as explained in section 4.3.

Switching our focus to the growth in perplexity as k increases, we tried to understand how the presence of attention mechanism impacts the ability of the neural architectures to model the ME-LDDs as k increases. For datasets with V=26, the impact of attention mechanism in Transformer-XL is apparent. The test perplexity score remains almost unchanged which we attribute to the presence of an attention mechanism. However, AWD-LSTM model struggles to maintain test perplexity scores as k increases, for datasets with V=26 (higher vocabulary size).

For datasets with V=4, it can be seen that the test perplexity of Transformer-XL model as a function of k scales exponentially. The presence of exponential relation indicates that the attention mechanism of the Transformer helps the model as k increases in the SPk grammar: the exponential relationship indicates that the growth in model's perplexity appears to saturate as k increases. For AWD-LSTM model, the test perplexity with k also increases at similar rate as that of Transformer-XL. This could be attributed to smaller vocabulary size, which leads to less complex dependency structure even at higher value of k. Such datasets could be easily modeled using

[3]The datasets and scripts used for training the models can be found at `https://github.com/silentknight/DelFol-ACL-2019`

non-attention mechanisms as seen in the figure 7.

Comparing the test perplexity scores in figure 7 for both of these models, it can be observed that the overall test perplexity score of Transformer-XL model for across all the datasets as compared with AWD-LSTM model is higher. This could be attributed to over-parameterization of the Transformer-XL model. Transformer-XL uses $\approx$44 million parameters as compared to $\approx$18 million used by AWD-LSTM model to model these sub-regular languages. It should also be noted that the height of the LDD characteristics of all the datasets is significantly lower than natural datasets (Mahalunkar and Kelleher, 2018). Consequently the mutual information is very small at a given distance D. This leads to higher perplexity in language models modeling them.

We also observed no apparent impact on the value of test perplexity scores of all the models on training sets with twice the number of strings. This can be substantiated by observing the LDD characteristics in section 4.5. Limitation of *foma* tool to generate datasets with various properties prevented us from exploring more complex datasets. *E.g.* we were unable to generate SP16 dataset with vocabulary size of V=26 due to *stack full* error.

6 Discussion

The LDD characteristics of a dataset is indicative of the presence of a certain type of grammar in the dataset. Our experiments reveal that even though a specific grammar does induce similar LDD characteristics, there are subtle variations. These variations depend on a number of factors such as size of the vocabulary, length of contextual relations, dependency structure (for e.g. "k" and "*forbidden subsequences*"). This analysis improves our understanding of the complex nature of the LDDs. This analysis can be extended to natural datasets in an effort to better understand the datasets. Thus, if a sequential model such as recurrent neural architecture intends to model a dataset, knowing these factors would greatly benefit in selecting the best hyper-parameters of the sequential model. By training Transformer-XL and AWD-LSTM model with datasets possessing various properties, it was possible to observe the impact of various properties on the perplexity score. Also, the impact of multi-head attention mechanism on the vocabulary size is quite evident. Our results suggest that the Transformer-XL performs much better with increase in vocabulary size. It is also evidenced by its SoTA results on *WikiText103* dataset (V=267735) (Dai* et al., 2019).

7 Conclusion

The majority of neural network research on sequential models focuses solely on modelling dependencies across long distances. However, the dependencies that occur in sequential data can also be multi-element. Furthermore, the vocabulary size, and the forbidden subsequences within a grammar also contribute to the difficulty of modelling the dependencies within a dataset.

In natural datasets all of these factors interact, and can confound the analysis for model performance. However, using SPk languages it is possible to synthesize sequential datasets and control the type of dependencies exhibited in these datasets. Using a mutual information based analysis of SPk synthesized datasets we examined how the different language characteristics (vocabulary size, forbidden subsequences) and dependency characteristics (length, k) are reflected in the datasets generated by SPk grammars. Furthermore, our results suggest that attention mechanisms in neural networks may aide in modeling datasets with multi-element long-distance dependencies. Although we encourage developing more efficient models.

The potential impact of this work for neural networks research include: an appreciation of the multifaceted nature of LDDs; a procedure for measuring LDD characteristics within a dataset; an understanding of how different hyper-parameters setting on an SPk based dataset synthesis process (string length, k, forbidden subsequences, vocabulary size) affect the mutual information profile of the resulting dataset.

Acknowledgment

This research was partly supported by the ADAPT Research Centre, funded under the SFI Research Centres Programme (Grant 13/RC/2106) and is co-funded under the European Regional Development Funds. The research was also supported by an IBM Shared University Research Award. We gratefully acknowledge the support of NVIDIA Corporation with the donation of the Titan Xp GPU under NVIDIA GPU Grant used for this research.

References

Enes Avcu, Chihiro Shibata, and Jeffrey Heinz. 2017. Subregular complexity and deep learning. In *Proceedings of the Conference on Logic and Machine Learning in Natural Language (LaML)*.

Gerlof Bouma. 2009. Normalized (pointwise) mutual information in collocation extraction.

M. Casey. 1996. The dynamics of discrete-time computation, with application to recurrent neural networks and finite state machine extraction. *Neural Computation*, 8(6):1135–1178.

N. Chomsky. 1956. Three models for the description of language. *IRE Transactions on Information Theory*, 2(3):113–124.

Noam Chomsky. 1959. On certain formal properties of grammars. *Information and Control*, 2(2):137–167.

Thomas M. Cover and Joy A. Thomas. 1991. *Elements of Information Theory*. Wiley-Interscience, New York, NY, USA.

Zihang Dai*, Zhilin Yang*, Yiming Yang, William W. Cohen, Jaime Carbonell, Quoc V. Le, and Ruslan Salakhutdinov. 2019. Transformer-XL: Language modeling with longer-term dependency.

Werner Ebeling and Thorsten Poeschel. 2002. Entropy and Long range correlations in literary English. 26(2):241–246.

W Tecumseh Fitch and Angela D Friederici. 2012. Artificial grammar learning meets formal language theory: an overview. *Philosophical Transactions of the Royal Society B: Biological Sciences*, 367(1598):1933–1955.

Jie Fu, Jeffrey Heinz, and Herbert G. Tanner. 2011. An algebraic characterization of strictly piecewise languages. *Lecture Notes in Computer Science (including subseries Lecture Notes in Artificial Intelligence and Lecture Notes in Bioinformatics)*, 6648 LNCS:252–263.

C. L. Giles, C. B. Miller, D. Chen, H. H. Chen, G. Z. Sun, and Y. C. Lee. 1992. Learning and extracting finite state automata with second-order recurrent neural networks. *Neural Computation*, 4(3):393–405.

P. Grassberger. 2003. Entropy Estimates from Insufficient Samplings. *ArXiv Physics e-prints*.

Jeffrey Heinz and James Rogers. 2010. Estimating strictly piecewise distributions. In *Proceedings of the 48th Annual Meeting of the Association for Computational Linguistics*, ACL '10, pages 886–896, Stroudsburg, PA, USA. Association for Computational Linguistics.

Sepp Hochreiter and Jürgen Schmidhuber. 1997. Long short-term memory. *Neural computation*, 9(8):1735–1780.

Mans Hulden. 2009. Foma: a finite-state compiler and library. In *Proceedings of the 12th Conference of the European Chapter of the Association for Computational Linguistics*, pages 29–32. Association for Computational Linguistics.

G. Jager and J. Rogers. 2012. Formal language theory: refining the Chomsky hierarchy. *Philosophical Transactions of the Royal Society B: Biological Sciences*, 367(1598):1956–1970.

Wentian Li. 1990. Mutual information functions versus correlation functions. *Journal of Statistical Physics*, 60(5):823–837.

Henry W. Lin and Max Tegmark. 2017. Critical behavior in physics and probabilistic formal languages. *Entropy*, 19(7).

Abhijit Mahalunkar and John D. Kelleher. 2018. Understanding Recurrent Neural Architectures by Analyzing and Synthesizing Long Distance Dependencies in Benchmark Sequential Datasets. *arXiv e-prints*, page arXiv:1810.02966.

Abhijit Mahalunkar and John D. Kelleher. 2018. Using regular languages to explore the representational capacity of recurrent neural architectures. In *Artificial Neural Networks and Machine Learning – ICANN 2018*, pages 189–198, Cham. Springer International Publishing.

Stephen Merity, Nitish Shirish Keskar, and Richard Socher. 2018. Regularizing and optimizing LSTM language models. In *International Conference on Learning Representations*.

Liam Paninski. 2003. Estimation of entropy and mutual information. *Neural Computation*, 15(6):1191–1253.

Arthur S. Reber. 1967. Implicit learning of artificial grammars. *Journal of Verbal Learning and Verbal Behavior*, 6(6):855–863.

James Rogers, Jeffrey Heinz, Gil Bailey, Matt Edlefsen, Molly Visscher, David Wellcome, and Sean Wibel. 2010. On Languages Piecewise Testable in the Strict Sense. In *The Mathematics of Language*, pages 255–265, Berlin, Heidelberg. Springer Berlin Heidelberg.

A. W. Smith and D. Zipser. 1989. Encoding sequential structure: experience with the real-time recurrent learning algorithm. In *International 1989 Joint Conference on Neural Networks*, pages 645–648 vol.1.

Masaru Tomita. 1982. Learning of construction of finite automata from examples using hill-climbing : RR : Regular set Recognizer. *Proceedings of Fourth International Cognitive Science Conference*, pages 105–108.

Raymond L. Watrous and Gary M. Kuhn. 1991. Induction of finite-state automata using second-order recurrent networks. In *NIPS*.

LSTM Networks Can Perform Dynamic Counting

Mirac Suzgun[1] **Sebastian Gehrmann**[1] **Yonatan Belinkov**[12] **Stuart M. Shieber**[1]

[1] Harvard John A. Paulson School of Engineering and Applied Sciences
[2] MIT Computer Science and Artificial Intelligence Laboratory
Cambridge, MA, USA
{msuzgun@college,{gehrmann,belinkov,shieber}@seas}.harvard.edu

Abstract

In this paper, we systematically assess the ability of standard recurrent networks to perform dynamic counting and to encode hierarchical representations. All the neural models in our experiments are designed to be small-sized networks both to prevent them from memorizing the training sets and to visualize and interpret their behaviour at test time. Our results demonstrate that the Long Short-Term Memory (LSTM) networks can learn to recognize the well-balanced parenthesis language (Dyck-1) and the shuffles of multiple Dyck-1 languages, each defined over different parenthesis-pairs, by emulating simple real-time k-counter machines. To the best of our knowledge, this work is the first study to introduce the shuffle languages to analyze the computational power of neural networks. We also show that a single-layer LSTM with only one hidden unit is practically sufficient for recognizing the Dyck-1 language. However, none of our recurrent networks was able to yield a good performance on the Dyck-2 language learning task, which requires a model to have a stack-like mechanism for recognition.

1 Introduction

Recurrent Neural Networks (RNNs) are known to capture long-distance and complex dependencies within sequential data. In recent years, RNN-based architectures have emerged as a powerful and effective architecture choice for language modeling (Mikolov et al., 2010). When equipped with infinite precision and rational state weights, RNN models are known to be theoretically Turing-complete (Siegelmann and Sontag, 1995). However, there still remain some fundamental questions regarding the practical computational expressivity of RNNs with finite precision.

Weiss et al. (2018) have recently demonstrated that Long Short-Term Memory (LSTM) models (Hochreiter and Schmidhuber, 1997), a popular variant of RNNs, can, theoretically, emulate a simple real-time k-counter machine, which can be described as a finite state controller with k separate counters, each containing integer values and capable of manipulating their content by adding ± 1 or 0 at each time step (Fischer et al., 1968). The authors further tested their theoretical result by training the LSTM networks to learn $a^n b^n$ and $a^n b^n c^n$. Their examination of the cell state dynamics of the models exhibited the existence of simple counting mechanisms in the cell states. Nonetheless, these two formal languages can be captured by a particularly simple form of automaton, a deterministic one-turn two-counter automaton (Ginsburg and Spanier, 1966). Hence, there is still an open question of whether the LSTMs can empirically learn to emulate more general finite-state automata equipped with multiple counters capable of performing an arbitrary number of turns.

In the present paper, we answer this question in the affirmative. We assess the empirical performance of three types of recurrent networks—Elman-RNNs (or RNNs, in short), LSTMs, and Gated Recurrent Units (GRUs)—to perform *dynamic counting* by training them to learn the Dyck-1 language. Our results demonstrate that the LSTMs with only a single hidden unit perform with perfect accuracy on the Dyck-1 learning task, and successfully generalize far beyond the training set. Furthermore, we show that the LSTMs can learn the shuffles of multiple Dyck-1 languages, defined over disjoint parenthesis-pairs, which require the emulation of multiple-counter arbitrary-turn machines. Our results corroborate the theoretical findings of Weiss et al. (2018), while extending their empirical observations. On the other hand, when trained to learn the Dyck-2 language, which is a strictly context-free language, all our recurrent models failed to learn the language.

Proceedings of the Workshop on Deep Learning and Formal Languages: Building Bridges, pages 44–54
Florence, Italy, August, 2nd 2019.

2 Preliminaries

We start by defining several subclasses of deterministic pushdown automata (DPA). Following Valiant and Paterson (1975), we define a deterministic one-counter automaton (DCA_1) to be a DPA with a stack alphabet consisting of only one symbol. Traditionally, this construction allows ϵ-moves (that is, executing actions on the stack without the observance of any inputs), but we restrict our attention to simple DCA_1s without ϵ-moves in the rest of this paper. Similarly, we call a DPA that contains k separate stacks, with each stack using only one stack symbol, a deterministic k-counter automaton (DCA_k).[1]

One can impose a further restriction on the direction of stack movement of a DPA. This notion leads to the definition of a deterministic n-turn pushdown automaton (or n-turn DPA, in short) and is well-studied by Ginsburg and Spanier (1966) and Valiant (1974): A DPA is said to be an n-turn DPA if the total number of direction changes in the stack movement of the DPA is at most n for each stack. Note that a one-turn DCA_1 can recognize $a^n b^n$ (Valiant, 1973), whereas a one-turn DCA_2 can recognize $a^n b^n c^n$. We say that a DCA_k with no limit on the number of turns can perform *dynamic counting*.

3 Related Work

Formal languages have long been used to demonstrate the computational power of neural networks. Early studies (Steijvers, 1996; Tonkes and Wiles, 1997; Rodriguez and Wiles, 1998; Bodén et al., 1999; Bodén and Wiles, 2000; Rodriguez, 2001) employed Elman-style RNNs (Elman, 1990) to recognize simple context-free and context-sensitive languages, such as $a^n b^n$, $a^n b^n c^n$, and $a^n b^n c b^m a^m$. Most of these architectures, however, suffered from the vanishing gradient problem (Hochreiter, 1998) and could not generalize far beyond their training sets.

Using LSTMs (Hochreiter and Schmidhuber, 1997), Gers and Schmidhuber (2001) showed that their models could learn two strictly context-free languages and one strictly context-sensitive language by effectively using their gating mechanisms. In contrast, Das et al. (1992) proposed an RNN model with an external stack memory, named Recurrent Neural Network Pushdown Automaton (NNPDA), to learn basic context-free grammars.

More recently, Joulin and Mikolov (2015) introduced simple RNN models equipped with differentiable stack modules, called Stack-RNN, to infer algorithmic patterns, and showed that their model could successfully learn various formal languages, in particular $a^n b^n$, $a^n b^n c^n$, $a^n b^n c^n d^n$, $a^n b^{2n}$. Inspired by the early model design of NNPDAs, Grefenstette et al. (2015) also proposed memory-augmented recurrent networks (Neural Stacks, Queues, and DeQues), which are RNNs equipped with unbounded differentiable memory modules, to perform sequence-to-sequence transduction tasks that require specific data structures.

Deleu and Dureau (2016) investigated the ability of Neural Turing Machines (NTMs; Graves et al. (2014)) to capture long-distance dependencies in the Dyck-1 language. Their empirical findings demonstrated that an NTM can recognize this language by emulating a DPA. Similarly, Sennhauser and Berwick (2018), Bernardy (2018), and Hao et al. (2018) conducted experiments on the Dyck languages to explore whether recurrent networks can learn nested structures. These studies assessed the performance of their recurrent models to predict the next possible parenthesis, assuming that it is a closing parenthesis.[2] In fact, Bernardy (2018) used a purpose-designed architecture, called RUSS, which contains recurrent units with stack-like states, to perform the closing-parenthesis-completion task. Though the RUSS model had no trouble generalizing to longer and deeper sequences, as the author mentions, the specificity of the architecture disqualifies it as a practical model choice for natural language modeling tasks. Additionally, Skachkova et al. (2018) trained recurrent networks to predict the last appropriate closing parenthesis, given a Dyck-2 sequence without its last symbol. They showed that their GRU and LSTM models performed with almost full accuracy on this parenthesis-completion task, but their task does not illustrate that these RNN models can recognize the Dyck language.

Most recently, Weiss et al. (2018) and Suzgun et al. (2019) showed that the LSTM networks can develop natural counting mechanisms to rec

[1] Weiss et al. (2018) call such a construction a k-counter machine. Previous papers provide a detailed investigation of the complexity of counting machines (Minsky, 1967; Fischer et al., 1968; Valiant and Paterson, 1975; Valiant, 1975).

[2] Their approach is slightly different than ours in the sense that we always try to predict the set of all the possible opening and closing parentheses at each time step.

ognize simple context-free and context-sensitive languages, particularly a^nb^n, $a^nb^nc^n$, $a^nb^nc^nd^n$. Their examination of the cell states of the LSTMs revealed that the models learned to emulate simple one- and two-turn counters to recognize these formal languages, but the authors did not conduct any experiments on tasks that require counters to perform arbitrary number of turns.

4 Models

All the models in this paper are recurrent neural architectures and known to capture long-distance relationships in sequential data. We would like to compare and contrast their ability to perform dynamic counting to recognize simple counting languages. We further investigate whether they can learn the Dyck-2 language by emulating a DPA.

A simple RNN architecture (Elman, 1990) is a recurrent model that takes an input x_t and a previous hidden state representation h_{t-1} to produce the next hidden state representation h_t, that is:

$$h_t = f(\mathbf{W}_{ih}x_t + \mathbf{b}_{ih} + \mathbf{W}_{hh}h_{t-1} + \mathbf{b}_{hh})$$
$$y_t = \sigma(\mathbf{W}_y h_t)$$

where $x_t \in \mathbb{R}^D$ is the input, $h_t \in \mathbb{R}^H$ the hidden state, $y_t \in \mathbb{R}^D$ the output at time t, $\mathbf{W}_y \in \mathbb{R}^{D \times H}$ the linear output layer, f an activation function[3] and σ an elementwise logistic sigmoid function.

In theory, it is known that RNNs with infinite precision and rational state weights are computationally universal models (Siegelmann and Sontag, 1995). However, in practice, the exact computational power of RNNs with finite precision is still unknown. Empirically, RNNs suffer from the vanishing or exploding gradient problem, as the length of the input sequences grow (Hochreiter, 1998). To address this issue, different neural architectures have been proposed over the years. Here, we focus on two popular RNN variants with similar gating mechanism, namely LSTMs and GRUs.

The LSTM model was introduced by Hochreiter and Schmidhuber (1997) to capture long-distance dependencies more accurately than simple RNNs. It contains additional gating components to facilitate the flow of gradients during back-propagation.

The GRU model was proposed by Cho et al. (2014) as an alternative to LSTM. GRUs are similar to LSTMs in their design, but do not contain an additional memory unit.

[3]In our experiments, we used the tanh function.

5 Experimental Setup

To evaluate the capability of RNN-based architectures to perform dynamic counting and to encode hierarchical representations, we conducted experiments on four different synthetic sequence prediction tasks. Each task was designed to highlight some particular feature of recurrent networks. All the tasks were formulated as supervised learning problems with discrete k-hot targets and mean-squared-error loss under the sequence prediction framework, defined next. We repeated each experiment ten times but used the same random seed across each run for each of the tasks to ensure comparability of RNN, GRU, and LSTM models.

5.1 The Sequence Prediction Task

Following Gers and Schmidhuber (2001), we trained the models as follows: Given a sequence in the language, we presented one character at each time step to the network and trained the network to predict the set of next possible characters in the language, based on the current input character and the prior hidden state. We used a one-hot representation to encode the inputs and a k-hot representation to encode the outputs. In all the experiments, the objective was to minimize the mean-squared error of the sequence predictions. We used an output threshold criterion of 0.5 for the sigmoid layer to indicate which characters were predicted by the model. Finally, we turned this sequence prediction task into a sequence classification task by *accepting* a sequence if the model predicted *all* of its output values correctly and *rejecting* it otherwise.

5.2 Training Details

Given the nature of the four languages that we will describe shortly, if recurrent models can learn them, then they should be able to do so with reasonably few hidden units and without the employment of any embedding layer or the dropout operation.[4] To that end, all the recurrent models used in our experiments were single-layer networks containing less than 10 hidden units. The number of hidden units that the networks contained for the Dyck-1, Dyck-2, Shuffle-2, and Shuffle-6 experiments were 3, 4, 4, and 8, respectively. (In Section 7, we describe further experiments with as few as a single hidden unit.) In all our experiments, we used the Adam optimizer (Kingma and Ba, 2014) with hyperparameter $\alpha = 0.001$.

[4]Some previous studies used embeddings (Sennhauser and Berwick, 2018; Bernardy, 2018) and the dropout oper-

Sample	(( )) ( ) ( )								([( )]) [([ ])] [ ]													
Input	(	(	)	)	(	)	(	)	(	[	(	)	]	)	[	(	[	]	)	]	[	]
Output	1	1	1	0	1	0	1	0	1	2	1	2	1	0	2	1	2	1	2	0	2	0

Table 1: Example input-output pairs for the Dyck-1 (left) and Dyck-2 (right) languages.

Sample	([( ))] [([ ]])												[{ ( ) }] ⟨ ⌈ ⌉ ⟩									
Input	(	[	(	)	)	]	[	(	[	]	]	)	[	{	(	)	}	]	⟨	⌈	⌉	⟩
Output	1	3	3	3	2	0	2	3	3	3	1	0	2	6	7	6	2	0	8	24	8	0

Table 2: Example input-output pairs for the Shuffle-2 (left) and Shuffle-6 (right) languages.

6 Experiments

The first language, Dyck-1 (or D_1), consists of well-balanced sequences of opening and closing parentheses. Recall that a neural network need not be equipped with a stack-like mechanism to recognize the Dyck-1 language under the sequence prediction paradigm; a single counter DCA_1 is sufficient. However, dynamic counting is required to capture the language.

The next two languages are the shuffles of two and six Dyck-1 languages, each defined over disjoint parentheses; we refer to these two languages as *Shuffle*-2 and *Shuffle*-6, respectively. These two tasks are formulated to investigate whether recurrent networks can emulate deterministic k-counter automata by performing dynamic counting, separately counting the number of opening and closing parentheses for each of the distinct parenthesis-pairs and predicting the closing parentheses for the pairs for which the counters are non-zero, in addition to the opening parentheses. In contrast, the final language, Dyck-2, is a context-free language which cannot be captured by a simple counting mechanism; a model capable of recognizing the Dyck-2 language must contain a stack-like component (Sennhauser and Berwick, 2018).

Tables 1 and 2 provide example input-output pairs for the four languages under the sequence-prediction task. For purposes of presentation only, we use a simple binary encoding of the output sets to concisely represent the output. In all of the languages we investigate in this paper, the open parentheses are always allowable as next symbol; we assign the set of open parentheses the number 0. Each closing parenthesis is assigned a different power of 2:) is assigned to 1,] to 2, } to 4, ⟩ to 8, ⌉ to 16, and ⌋ to 32. (These latter closing parentheses are needed for the Shuffle-6 language below.) The set of predicted symbols is then the sum of the associated numbers. For instance, an output 3 represents the prediction of any of the open parentheses as well as) and].

We note that even though an input sequence might appear in two different languages, it might have different target representations. This observation is important especially when making comparisons between the Dyck-2 and the Shuffle-2 languages. For instance, the output sequence for ([ ]) in the Dyck-2 language is 1 2 1 0, whereas the output sequence for ([ ]) in the Shuffle-2 language is 1 3 1 0.

6.1 The Dyck-1 Language

The Dyck-1 language, or the well-balanced parenthesis language, arises naturally in enumerative combinatorics, statistics, and formal language theory. A sequence in the Dyck-1 language needs to contain an equal number of opening and closing parentheses, with the constraint that at each time step the total number of opening parentheses must be greater than or equal to the total number of closing parentheses so far. In other words, for a given sequence $s = s_1 \cdots s_{2n}$ of length $2n$ in the Dyck-1 language over the alphabet $\Sigma = \{(,)\}$, if we have a function f that assigns value $+1$ to '(' and value -1 to ')', then we know that it is always true that $\sum_{i=1}^{j} f(s_i) \geq 0$ with strict equality when $j = 2n$, for all $j \in [1, \ldots, 2n]$. Therefore, a model with a single unbounded counter can recognize this language.

A probabilistic context-free grammar for the Dyck-1 language can be written as follows:

$$S \rightarrow \begin{cases} (S) & \text{with probability } p \\ SS & \text{with probability } q \\ \varepsilon & \text{with probability } 1-(p+q) \end{cases}$$

where $0 < p, q < 1$ and $(p+q) < 1$.

ation (Bernardy, 2018) in their experiments.

Task	Model	Training Set Min	Training Set Max	Training Set Med	Short Test Set Min	Short Test Set Max	Short Test Set Med	Long Test Set Min	Long Test Set Max	Long Test Set Med
Dyck-1	RNN	0.45	76.17	46.96	0.28	73.62	41.89	0.06	24.44	7.19
Dyck-1	GRU	99.37	100	100	99.34	100	100	67.68	95.58	84.38
Dyck-1	**LSTM**	**100**	**100**	**100**	**100**	**100**	**100**	**99.98**	**100**	**100**
Shuffle-2	RNN	33.68	87.77	58.16	29.42	86.48	55.37	0.54	25.58	2.75
Shuffle-2	GRU	99.73	100	99.97	99.62	99.98	99.93	83.70	95.18	93.12
Shuffle-2	**LSTM**	**100**	**100**	**100**	**100**	**100**	**100**	**96.84**	**99.98**	**99.35**
Shuffle-6	RNN	0.26	57.39	44.54	0.16	54.80	41.38	0	0.64	0.15
Shuffle-6	GRU	96.32	99.98	99.78	96.08	99.98	99.81	51.96	97.30	85.14
Shuffle-6	**LSTM**	**99.68**	**100**	**100**	**99.74**	**100**	**100**	**82.92**	**99.72**	**98.14**
Dyck-2	RNN	4.37	31.67	14.74	2.96	27.46	12.21	0	0.46	0.01
Dyck-2	GRU	7.78	53.34	28.71	5.38	49.06	25.08	0	1.56	0.05
Dyck-2	**LSTM**	**19.76**	**52.13**	**35.82**	**16.58**	**48.24**	**31.29**	**0**	**1.46**	**0.20**

Table 3: The performances of the RNN, GRU, and LSTM models on four language modeling tasks. Shuffle-2 denotes the shuffle of two Dyck-1 languages defined over different alphabets, and similarly Shuffle-6 denotes the shuffle of six Dyck-1 languages defined over different alphabets. Min/Max/Median results were obtained from 10 different runs of each model with the same random seed across each run. We note that the LSTM models not only outperformed the RNN and GRU models but also often achieved full accuracy on the short test set in all the "counting" tasks. Nevertheless, even the LSTMs were not able to yield a good performance on the Dyck-2 language modeling task, which requires a stack-like mechanism.

Setting $p = \frac{1}{2}$ and $q = \frac{1}{4}$, we generated $10,000$ distinct Dyck sequences, whose lengths were bounded to $[2, 50]$, for the training set. We used two test sets: The "short" test set contained $5,000$ distinct Dyck words defined in the same length interval as the training set but distinct from it. The "long" test set contained $5,000$ distinct Dyck words defined in the interval $[52, 100]$. Hence, there was no overlap between any of the training and test sets.

Results: Table 3 lists the performances of the RNN, GRU, and LSTM models on the Dyck-1 language. First, we highlight that all the LSTM models obtained full accuracy on the training set and short test set, whose sequences were bounded to $[2, 50]$, in all the ten trials. They were also able to easily generalize to longer and deeper sequences in the long test set: They obtained perfect accuracy in nine out of ten trials and 99.98% accuracy (only 1 incorrect prediction) in the remaining trial. These results exhibit that the LSTMs can indeed perform unbounded dynamic counting.

The GRUs yielded an almost similar qualitative performance on the training and first test sets; however, they could not generalize well to longer and deeper sequences. On the other hand, the RNN models performed significantly worse than the first two recurrent models, in terms of their median accuracy rate. We note that similar empirical observations about the performance-level differences between the RNNs, GRUs, and LSTMs for other simple formal languages were also reported by Weiss et al. (2018) and Bernardy (2018).

6.2 The Shuffle-k Language

Next, we consider two *shuffle* languages, which are both generated by the Dyck-1 language. Before describing each task in detail, let us first define the notion of *shuffling* formally. The shuffling operation $|| : \Sigma^* \times \Sigma^* \to \mathcal{P}(\Sigma^*)$ can be inductively defined as follows:[5]

- $u||\varepsilon = \varepsilon||u = \{u\}$
- $\alpha u||\beta v = \alpha(u||\beta v) \cup \beta(\alpha u||v)$

for any $\alpha, \beta \in \Sigma$ and $u, v \in \Sigma^*$. For instance, the shuffling of ab and cd would be:

$$ab||cd = \{abcd, acbd, acdb, cabd, cadb, cdab\}$$

There is a natural extension of the shuffling operation $||$ to languages. The *shuffle* of two languages $\mathcal{L}_1$ and $\mathcal{L}_2$, denoted $\mathcal{L}_1||\mathcal{L}_2$, is defined as the set of all the possible interleavings of the elements of $\mathcal{L}_1$ and $\mathcal{L}_2$, respectively, that is:

$$\mathcal{L}_1||\mathcal{L}_2 = \bigcup_{u \in \mathcal{L}_1,\ v \in \mathcal{L}_2} u||v$$

[5]We abuse notation by allowing a string to stand for its own singleton set.

Given a language $\mathcal{L}$, we define its self-shuffling $\mathcal{L}||^2$ to be $\mathcal{L}||\sigma(\mathcal{L})$, where σ is an isomorphism on the vocabulary of $\mathcal{L}$ to a disjoint vocabulary. More generally, we define the k-self-shuffling

$$\mathcal{L}||^k = \begin{cases} \{\varepsilon\} & \text{if } k = 0 \\ \mathcal{L}||\sigma(\mathcal{L}||^{k-1}) & \text{otherwise} \end{cases} .$$

The Shuffle-2 Language: The first language is $D_1||^2$, the shuffle of D_1 and D_1, where the first D_1 is over the alphabet $\{(,)\}$ and the second over the alphabet $\{[,]\}$. For instance, the sequence ([ )] is in $D_1||^2$ but not in D_2, whereas ( ] [ ) is in neither $D_1||^2$ nor D_2. Note that D_2 is a subset of $D_1||^2$, but not the other way around.[6]

To generate the training and test corpora, we used a probabilistic context-free grammar for the Dyck-2 language, which we will describe shortly, but considered correct target values for the sequences interpreted as per the Shuffle-2 language. The training set contained $10,000$ distinct sequences of lengths in $[2, 50]$. As before, the short test set had $5,000$ distinct samples defined over the same length interval but disjoint from the training set, and the long test set had $5,000$ distinct samples, whose lengths were bounded to $[52, 100]$.

The Shuffle-6 Language: The second shuffle language is $D_1||^6$, the shuffle of six Dyck-1 languages, each defined over different parenthesis-pairs. Concretely, we used the following pairs: ( ), [ ], { }, ⟨ ⟩, ⌈ ⌉, ⌊ ⌋. In theory, an automaton with six separate unbounded-turn counters (DCA$_6$) can recognize this language. Hence, we wanted to explore whether our recurrent networks can learn to emulate a dynamic-counting 6-counter machine.

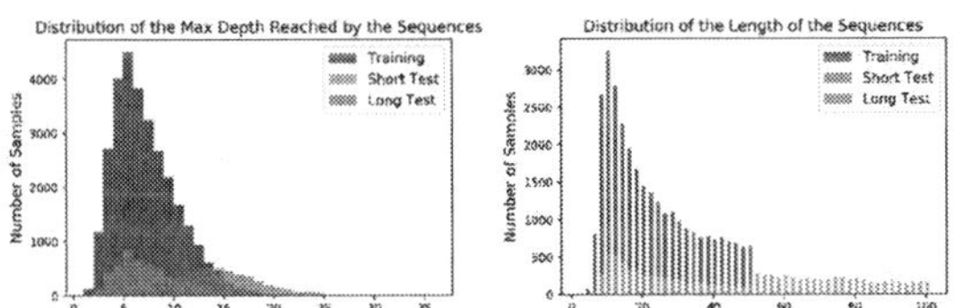

Figure 1: Length and maximum depth distributions of training/test sets for an example Shuffle-6 experiment.

The training and two test corpora were generated in the same style as the previous sequence prediction task; however, we included $30,000$ samples in the training set for this language, due to the complexity of the language. Figure 1 shows the length and maximum depth distributions of the training and test sets for one of the Shuffle-6 experiments.

Results: As shown shown in Table 3, the LSTM models achieved a median accuracy of 100% on the training and short test sets in both of the shuffle language variants. Furthermore, they were able to generalize well to longer and deeper sequences in both shuffle languages, achieving an almost perfect median accuracy score on the long test set. In contrast, the GRU models performed slightly worse than the LSTM models on the training and short test sets, but the GRUs did not yield the same performance as the LSTMs on the long test set, obtaining median scores of 93.12% and 85.14% in the Shuffle-2 and Shuffle-6 languages, respectively. Additionally, the simple RNN models always performed much worse than the GRU and LSTM models and could not even learn the training sets in either of the shuffle languages. These empirical findings show that the LSTM models can successfully emulate a DCA$_k$, a deterministic (real-time) automaton with k-counters, each capable of performing an arbitrary number of turns.

6.3 The Dyck-2 Language

The generalized Dyck language, D_n, represents the core of the notion of context-freeness by virtue of the Characterization Theorem of Chomsky and Schützenberger (1963), which provides a natural way to characterize the CFL class:

Theorem 6.1. *Any language in CFL can be represented as a homomorphic image of the intersection of a Dyck language D_n and a regular language R.*

Furthermore, D_n can be reduced to D_2 at the expense of increasing the depth and length of the original sequences in the former language.

Proposition 6.2. *D_n is reducible to D_2.*

Proof. [7] Let D_n be the Dyck language with n distinct pairs of parentheses. Let us further suppose that $p = \{p_1, p_2, p_3, \ldots, p_n\}$ are the opening parentheses and that $\bar{p} = \{\overline{p_1}, \overline{p_2}, \overline{p_3}, \ldots, \overline{p_n}\}$ are their corresponding closing parentheses. We set $m = \lceil \log_2 n \rceil$ and encode each opening and closing parenthesis in D_n with m bits using either (and [or) and]. Furthermore, we map empty string to empty string.

[6] On the other hand, we highlight once again that the target sequences in $D_1||^2$ are often different from those in D_2.

[7] A similar reduction is also provided by Magniez et al. (2014).

Given an open parenthesis p_i, we first determine the m-digit binary representation of the number $i-1$ and then use (to encode 0's and [to encode 1's in this representation. Given a closing parenthesis $\overline{p_i}$, we determine the m-digit binary representation of the number $i-1$, write the binary number *in the reverse order*, and then use) to encode 0's and] to encode 1's. That is,

$$\begin{aligned}\Gamma : p \cup \bar{p} \cup \{\varepsilon\} &\rightarrow \mathbb{S}^m \cup \{\varepsilon\} \\ p_i &\mapsto \mathbf{Enc}_{([} \circ \mathrm{Bin}(i-1) \\ \overline{p_i} &\mapsto \mathbf{Enc}_{)]} \circ \mathrm{Rev} \circ \mathrm{Bin}(i-1) \\ \varepsilon &\mapsto \varepsilon\end{aligned}$$

where $\mathbb{S} = \{(, [,),]\}$, the parentheses in D_2. We note that $s = s_1 s_2 s_3 \cdots s_k$ is in D_n if and only if $\Gamma(s) = \Gamma(s_1)\Gamma(s_2)\Gamma(s_3)\cdots\Gamma(s_k)$ is in D_2, completing the reduction. □

The previous proposition simply shows that we can map an expression in D_n to an expression in D_2 at the expense of creating a deeper structure in the latter language by a factor of $m = \lceil \log_2 n \rceil$. For instance, if an expression s in D_n has a maximum depth of k, then the expression generated by the mapping above would have a maximum depth of $k \times m$ in D_2.

Motivated by context-free-language universality (Sennhauser and Berwick, 2018), we therefore experimented with the Dyck-2 language defined over two types of parenthesis-pairs, namely $\{(,)\}$ and $\{[,]\}$, as well. The recognition of the Dyck-2 language requires a model to possess a stack-like component; real-time primitive counting does not enable us to capture the Dyck-2 language. Hence, if an RNN-based architecture learns to recognize this language, we can conclude that RNNs with finite precision can actually learn complex deeply nested representations.

A probabilistic context-free grammar for the Dyck-2 language can be written as follows:

$$S \rightarrow \begin{cases} (S) & \text{with probability } \frac{p}{2} \\ [S] & \text{with probability } \frac{p}{2} \\ SS & \text{with probability } q \\ \varepsilon & \text{with probability } 1-(p+q) \end{cases}$$

where $0 < p, q < 1$ and $(p+q) < 1$.

Setting $p = \frac{1}{2}$ and $q = \frac{1}{4}$, we generated $10,000$ distinct sequences, whose lengths were bounded to $[2, 50]$, for the training set. Again, we generated $5,000$ other distinct Dyck-2 sequences of lengths defined in the interval $[2, 50]$ for the first test set and $5,000$ distinct sequences of lengths defined in the interval $[52, 100]$ for the second test set. As in the previous case, there was no overlap between the training and test sets.

Results: As shown in Table 3, we found that none of our RNNs was able to emulate a DPA to recognize the Dyck-2 language, a context-free language that requires a model to contain a stack-like mechanism for recognition. Overall, the LSTM models had the best performances among all the networks, but they still failed to employ a stack-based strategy to learn the Dyck-2 language. Even the best LSTM model could achieve only 48.24% and 1.46% accuracy scores on the short and long test sets, respectively.

7 Discussion and Analysis

7.1 Visualization of Hidden+Cell States

Our empirical results on the Dyck-1 and Shuffle languages suggest that our LSTM models were performing dynamic counting to recognize these languages. In order to validate our hypothesis, we visualized the hidden and cell states of some of our LSTM models that achieved full accuracy on the test sets.

Figure 2 illustrates that our LSTM is able to recognize the samples in $D_1||^6$ by emulating a DCA_6. In fact, the discrete even transitions in the cell state dynamics of the model reveal that six out of eight hidden units in the model are acting like separate counters. In some cases, we further discovered that certain units learned to count the length of the input sequences. Such length counting behaviours are also observed in machine translation (Shi et al., 2016; Bau et al., 2019; Dalvi et al., 2019) when the LSTMs are trained on a fixed-length training corpus.[8]

On the other hand, Figure 3 provides visualizations of the hidden and cell state dynamics of one of our single-layer LSTM models with four hidden units when the model was presented two sequences in the Dyck-2 language. Both sequences have some noticeable patterns and were chosen to explore whether the model behaves differently in repeated (or similar) subsequences. It seems that the LSTM model is trying to employ a complex counting strategy to learn the Dyck-2 language but failing to accomplish this task.

[8]The visualizations for the Dyck-1 and Shuffle-2 languages were qualitatively similar.

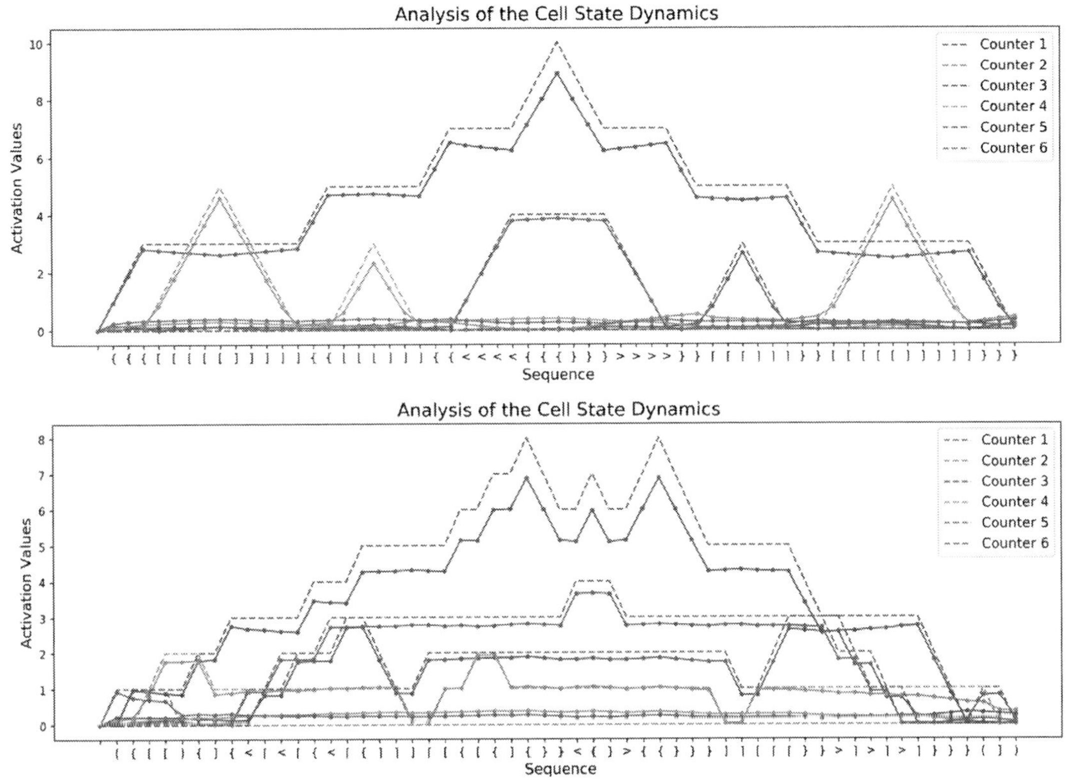

Figure 2: Visualization of the cell state dynamics of one of the LSTM models trained to learn $D_1||^6$, the Shuffle-6 language. The solid lines show the values of the cell states of the six out of eight units in the model, whereas the dashed lines depict the current depth of each distinct parenthesis-pair in $D_1||^6$. We highlight the striking parallelism between the solid lines and the dashed-lines. Our visualizations confirm that the LSTM models employ a simple counting mechanism to recognize the Shuffle languages.

7.2 LSTM with a Single Hidden Unit

In theory, a DCA_1 should be able to easily recognize Dyck-1, the well-balanced parenthesis language. Can an LSTM with one hidden unit learn Dyck-1? Our empirical results (Figure 4) confirmed that LSTMs can indeed learn this language by effectively using the single hidden unit to count up the total number of left and right parentheses in the sequence. Similarly, we found that an LSTM with only two hidden units can recognize $D_1||^2$.

7.3 Predicting the Last Closing Parenthesis

Following Skachkova et al. (2018), we also trained an LSTM model with four hidden units to learn to predict the last closing parenthesis in the Dyck-2 language. The model learned the task in a couple of epochs and achieved perfect accuracy on the training and test sets. However, our simple analysis of the cell state dynamics of the LSTM in Figure 5 suggests that the model is doing some complex form of counting to perform the desired task, rather than learning the Dyck-2 language.

8 Conclusion

We investigated the ability of standard recurrent networks to perform dynamic counting and to encode hierarchical representations, by considering three simple counting languages and the Dyck-2 language. Our empirical results highlight the overall high-caliber performance of the LSTM models over the simple RNNs and GRUs, and further inflect our understanding of the limitations and strengths of these models.

9 Acknowledgement

The first author gratefully acknowledges the support of the Harvard College Research Program (HCRP). The third author was supported by the Harvard Mind, Brain, and Behavior Initiative. The computations in this paper were run on the Odyssey cluster supported by the FAS Division of Science, Research Computing Group at Harvard University.

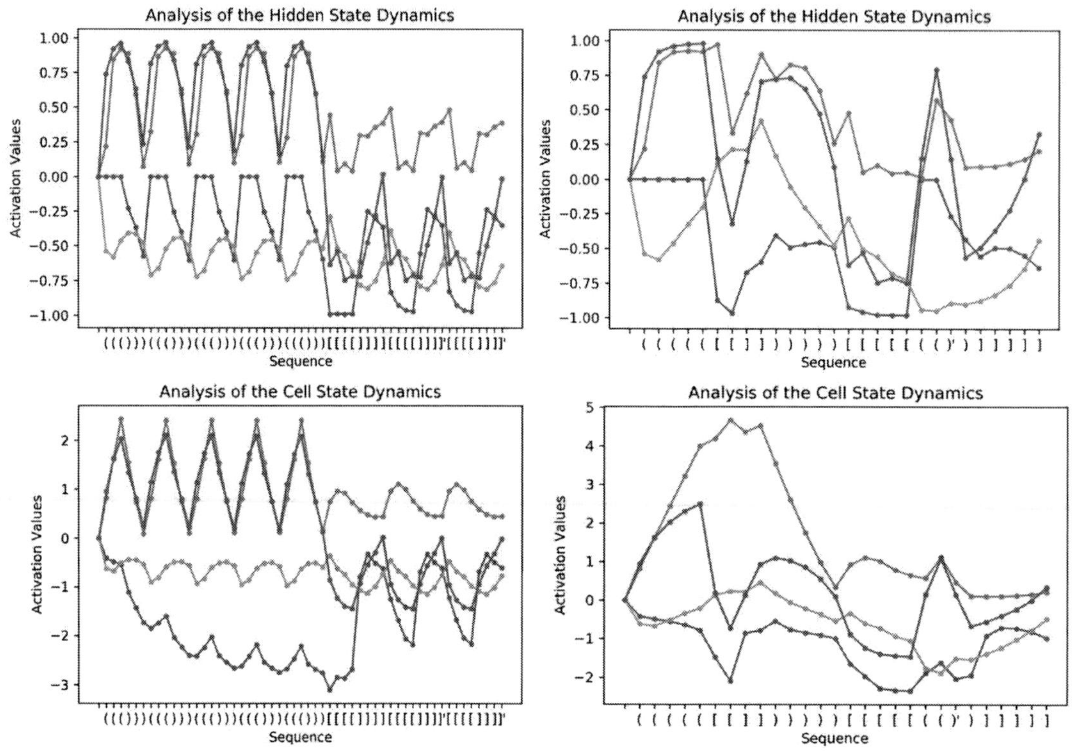

Figure 3: Visualization of the hidden and cell state dynamics of one of the LSTMs trained to learn the Dyck-2 language. The time steps at which the model made incorrect predictions are marked with an apostrophe in the horizontal axis. The plots on the left provide a demonstration of the periodic behaviour of the hidden and cell states of the model for a long sequence. Similarly, the plots on the right provide the complex counting behaviour of the model as it observes a nested sequence. We witnessed similar behaviours in our other models as well.

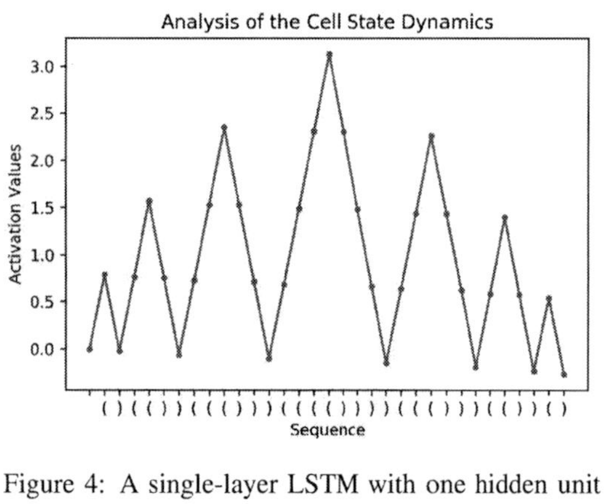

Figure 4: A single-layer LSTM with one hidden unit learns the Dyck-1 language by counting up upon the observance of (and down upon the observance of).

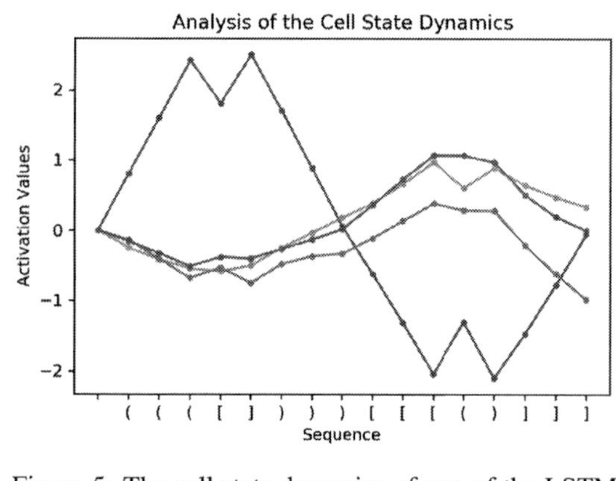

Figure 5: The cell state dynamics of one of the LSTM models trained to predict the last closing parenthesis. Our LSTMs often achieved full accuracy on this task.

References

Anthony Bau, Yonatan Belinkov, Hassan Sajjad, Nadir Durrani, Fahim Dalvi, and James Glass. 2019. Identifying and controlling important neurons in neural machine translation. In *International Conference on Learning Representations*.

Jean-Philippe Bernardy. 2018. Can recurrent neural networks learn nested recursion? *LiLT (Linguistic Issues in Language Technology)*, 16(1).

Mikael Bodén and Janet Wiles. 2000. Context-free and context-sensitive dynamics in recurrent neural networks. *Connection Science*, 12(3-4):197–210.

Mikael Bodén, Janet Wiles, Bradley Tonkes, and Alan Blair. 1999. Learning to predict a context-free language: Analysis of dynamics in recurrent hidden units.

Kyunghyun Cho, Bart Van Merriënboer, Caglar Gulcehre, Dzmitry Bahdanau, Fethi Bougares, Holger Schwenk, and Yoshua Bengio. 2014. Learning phrase representations using RNN encoder-decoder for statistical machine translation. *arXiv preprint arXiv:1406.1078*.

Noam Chomsky and Marcel P Schützenberger. 1963. The algebraic theory of context-free languages. In *Studies in Logic and the Foundations of Mathematics*, volume 35, pages 118–161. Elsevier.

Fahim Dalvi, Nadir Durrani, Hassan Sajjad, Yonatan Belinkov, D. Anthony Bau, and James Glass. 2019. What is one grain of sand in the desert? analyzing individual neurons in deep NLP models. In *Proceedings of the Thirty-Third AAAI Conference on Artificial Intelligence*.

Sreerupa Das, C Lee Giles, and Guo-Zheng Sun. 1992. Learning context-free grammars: Capabilities and limitations of a recurrent neural network with an external stack memory. In *Proceedings of The Fourteenth Annual Conference of Cognitive Science Society. Indiana University*, page 14.

Tristan Deleu and Joseph Dureau. 2016. Learning operations on a stack with Neural Turing Machines. *arXiv preprint arXiv:1612.00827*.

Jeffrey L Elman. 1990. Finding structure in time. *Cognitive science*, 14(2):179–211.

Patrick C Fischer, Albert R Meyer, and Arnold L Rosenberg. 1968. Counter machines and counter languages. *Mathematical systems theory*, 2(3):265–283.

Felix A Gers and E Schmidhuber. 2001. LSTM recurrent networks learn simple context-free and context-sensitive languages. *IEEE Transactions on Neural Networks*, 12(6):1333–1340.

Seymour Ginsburg and Edwin H Spanier. 1966. Finite-turn pushdown automata. *SIAM Journal on Control*, 4(3):429–453.

Alex Graves, Greg Wayne, and Ivo Danihelka. 2014. Neural Turing Machines. *arXiv preprint arXiv:1410.5401*.

Edward Grefenstette, Karl Moritz Hermann, Mustafa Suleyman, and Phil Blunsom. 2015. Learning to transduce with unbounded memory. In *Advances in Neural Information Processing Systems*, pages 1828–1836.

Yiding Hao, William Merrill, Dana Angluin, Robert Frank, Noah Amsel, Andrew Benz, and Simon Mendelsohn. 2018. Context-free transductions with neural stacks. *arXiv preprint arXiv:1809.02836*.

Sepp Hochreiter. 1998. The vanishing gradient problem during learning recurrent neural nets and problem solutions. *International Journal of Uncertainty, Fuzziness and Knowledge-Based Systems*, 6(02):107–116.

Sepp Hochreiter and Jürgen Schmidhuber. 1997. Long Short-Term Memory. *Neural computation*, 9(8):1735–1780.

Armand Joulin and Tomas Mikolov. 2015. Inferring algorithmic patterns with stack-augmented recurrent nets. In *Advances in neural information processing systems*, pages 190–198.

Diederik P Kingma and Jimmy Ba. 2014. Adam: A method for stochastic optimization. *arXiv preprint arXiv:1412.6980*.

Frédéric Magniez, Claire Mathieu, and Ashwin Nayak. 2014. Recognizing well-parenthesized expressions in the streaming model. *SIAM Journal on Computing*, 43(6):1880–1905.

Tomáš Mikolov, Martin Karafiát, Lukáš Burget, Jan Černockỳ, and Sanjeev Khudanpur. 2010. Recurrent neural network based language model. In *Eleventh annual conference of the international speech communication association*.

Marvin Lee Minsky. 1967. *Computation: Finite and Infinite Machines*. Prentice-Hall Englewood Cliffs.

Paul Rodriguez. 2001. Simple recurrent networks learn context-free and context-sensitive languages by counting. *Neural computation*, 13(9):2093–2118.

Paul Rodriguez and Janet Wiles. 1998. Recurrent neural networks can learn to implement symbol-sensitive counting. In *Advances in Neural Information Processing Systems*, pages 87–93.

Luzi Sennhauser and Robert Berwick. 2018. Evaluating the ability of LSTMs to learn context-free grammars. In *Proceedings of the 2018 EMNLP Workshop BlackboxNLP: Analyzing and Interpreting Neural Networks for NLP*, pages 115–124.

Xing Shi, Kevin Knight, and Deniz Yuret. 2016. Why neural translations are the right length. In *Proceedings of the 2016 Conference on Empirical Methods in Natural Language Processing*, pages 2278–2282.

Hava T Siegelmann and Eduardo D Sontag. 1995. On the computational power of neural nets. *Journal of computer and system sciences*, 50(1):132–150.

Natalia Skachkova, Thomas Trost, and Dietrich Klakow. 2018. Closing brackets with recurrent neural networks. In *Proceedings of the 2018 EMNLP Workshop BlackboxNLP: Analyzing and Interpreting Neural Networks for NLP*, pages 232–239.

Mark Steijvers. 1996. A recurrent network that performs a context-sensitive prediction task.

Mirac Suzgun, Yonatan Belinkov, and Stuart M Shieber. 2019. On evaluating the generalization of LSTM models in formal languages. *Proceedings of the Society for Computation in Linguistics (SCiL)*, pages 277–286.

Bradley Tonkes and Janet Wiles. 1997. Learning a context-free task with a recurrent neural network: An analysis of stability. In *In Proceedings of the Fourth Biennial Conference of the Australasian Cognitive Science Society*. Citeseer.

Leslie Valiant. 1973. *Decision Procedures for Families of Deterministic Pushdown Automata*. Ph.D. thesis, University of Warwick.

Leslie G Valiant. 1974. The equivalence problem for deterministic finite-turn pushdown automata. *Information and Control*, 25(2):123–133.

Leslie G Valiant. 1975. Regularity and related problems for deterministic pushdown automata. *Journal of the ACM (JACM)*, 22(1):1–10.

Leslie G Valiant and Michael S Paterson. 1975. Deterministic one-counter automata. *Journal of Computer and System Sciences*, 10(3):340–350.

Gail Weiss, Yoav Goldberg, and Eran Yahav. 2018. On the practical computational power of finite precision RNNs for language recognition. In *Proceedings of the 56th Annual Meeting of the Association for Computational Linguistics (Volume 2: Short Papers)*, pages 740–745.

Author Index

Arkoudas, Konstantine, 14

Belinkov, Yonatan, 44

Gehrmann, Sebastian, 44
Grzes, Marek, 24

Kelleher, John, 34

Liza, Farhana Ferdousi, 24

Mahalunkar, Abhijit, 34
Merrill, William, 1

Shieber, Stuart, 44
Suzgun, Mirac, 44

Teichmann, Christoph, 14

Xiao, Chunyang, 14

Association for Computational Linguistics
209 N. Eighth Street
Stroudsburg, Pennsylvania 18360

ISBN 978-1-5108-9118-0

CURRAN ASSOCIATES INC.
proceedings.com